NOT MY SHAME

T.O.Walker

SINGING
DRAGON

There's something
really empowering
about telling
your own story

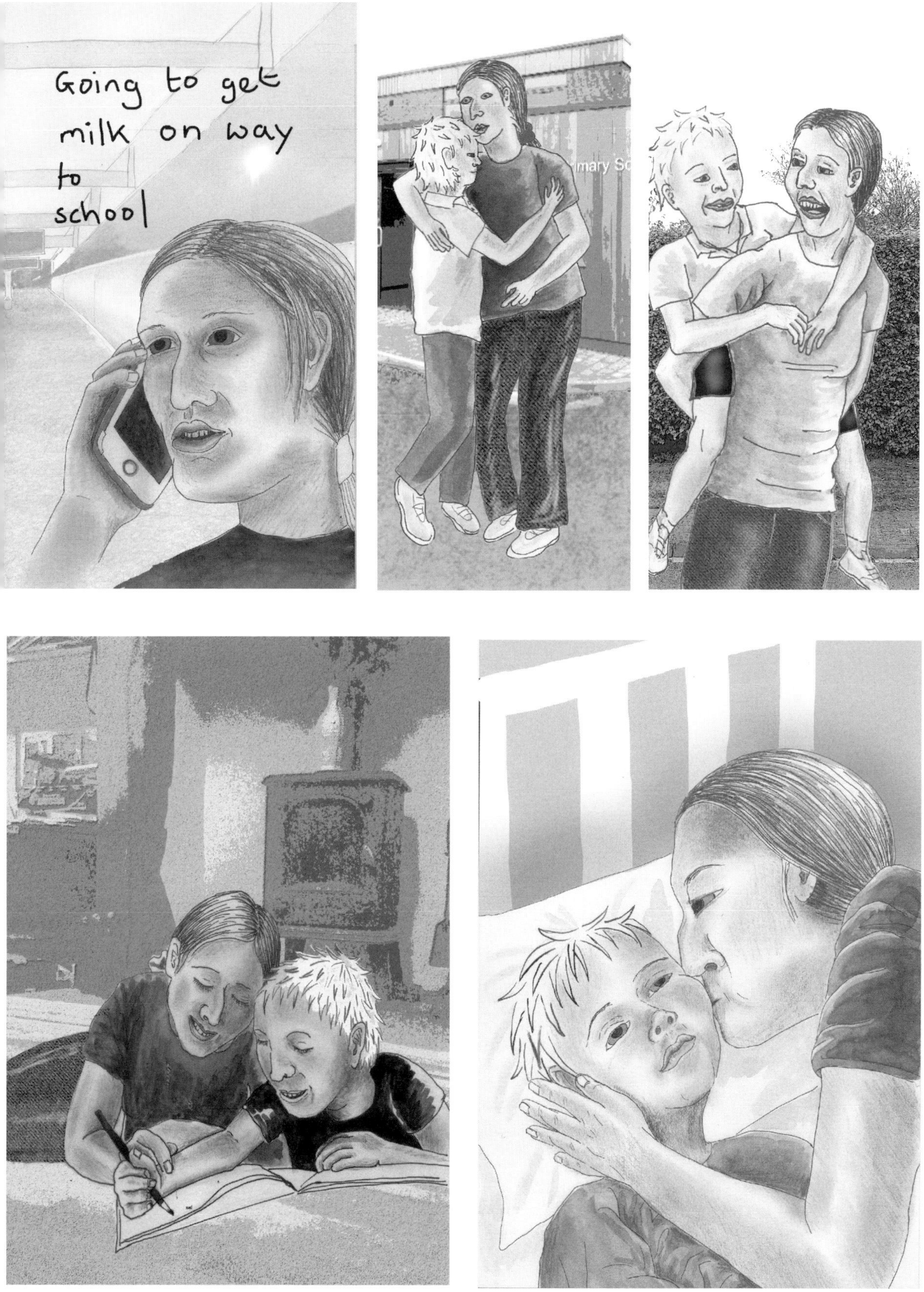
Going to get milk on way to school

I sat down
to read the
paper and
this happened
. . .

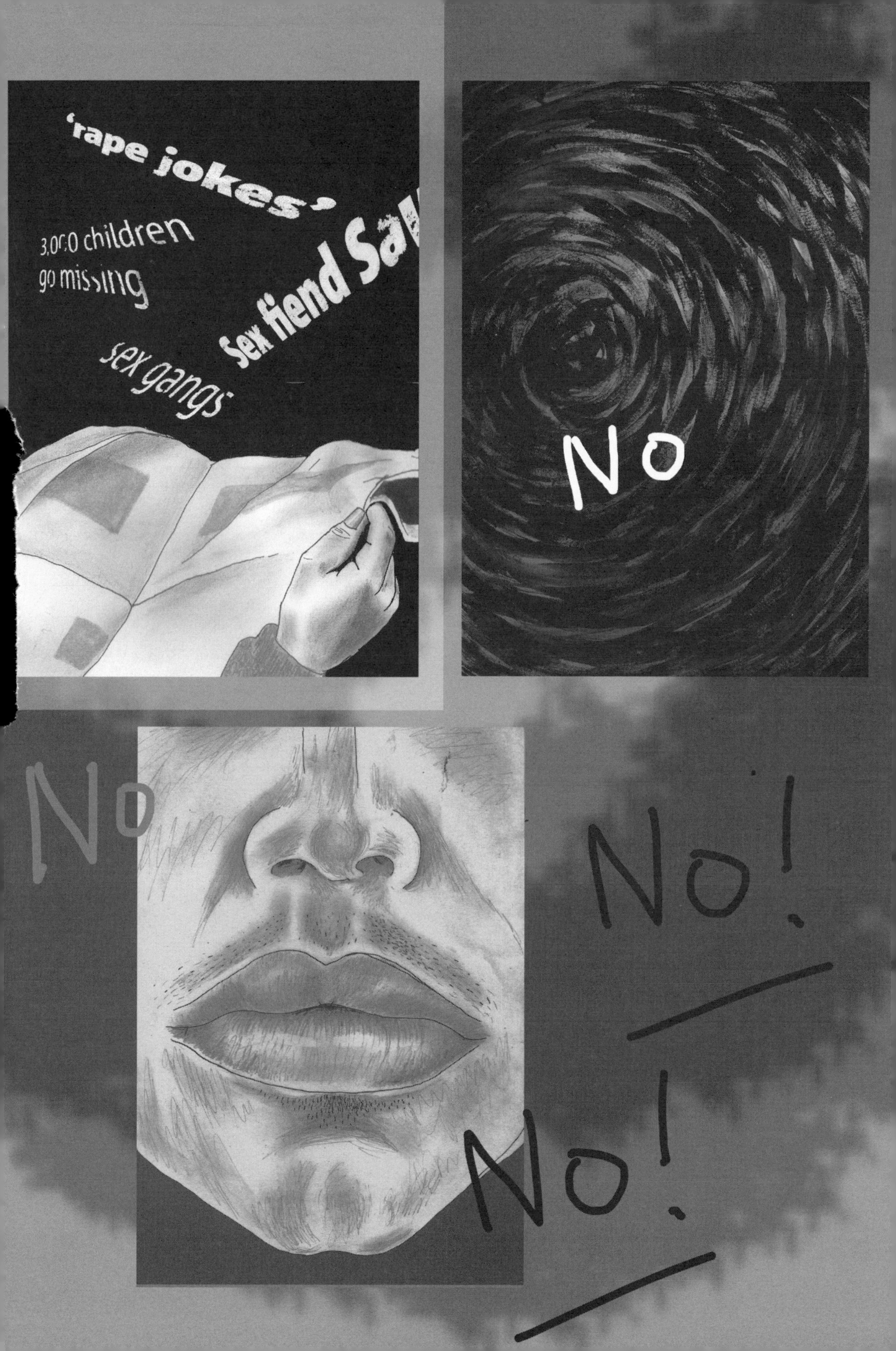
'rape jokes'
3,000 children
go missing
Sex fiend
sex gangs
No
No
No!
No!

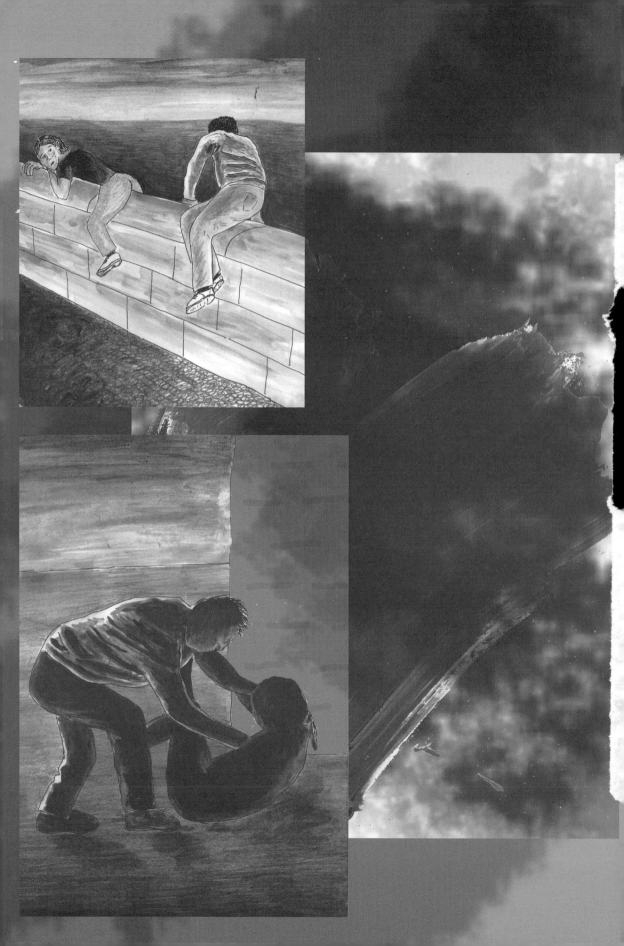

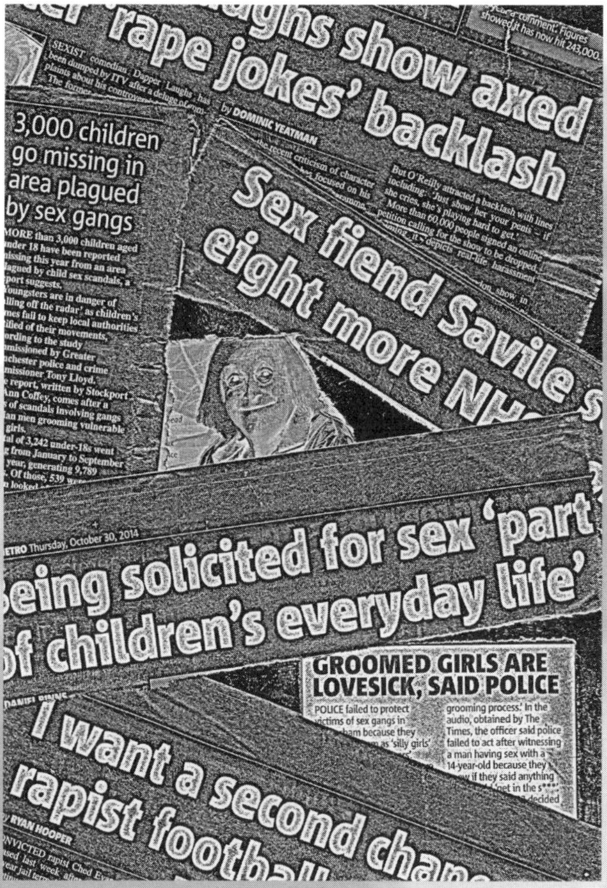
'rape jokes' backlash
show axed
3,000 children go missing in area plagued by sex gangs
Sex fiend Savile
eight more NHS
Being solicited for sex 'part of children's everyday life'
GROOMED GIRLS ARE LOVESICK, SAID POLICE
I want a second chance
rapist football

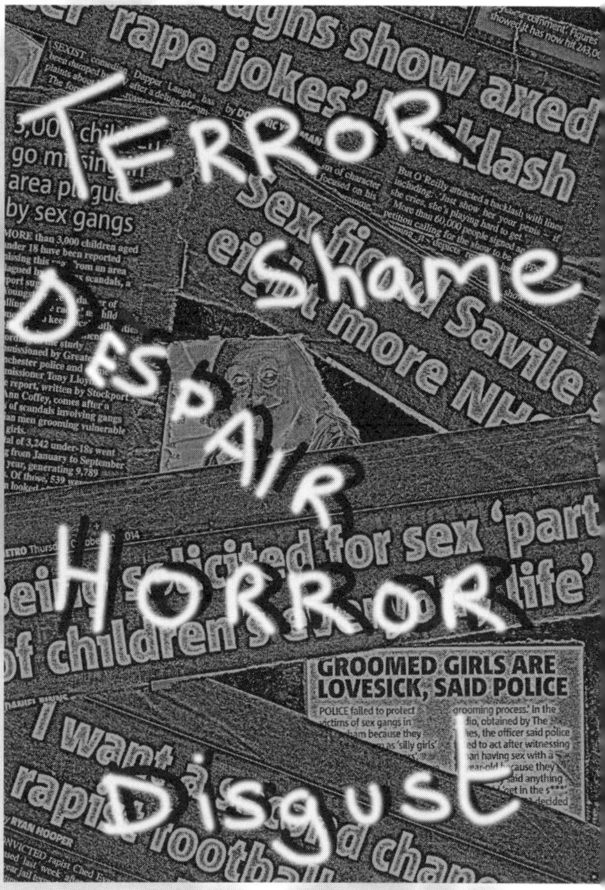
TERROR
Shame
DESPAIR
HORROR
Disgust

and
suddenly
I am
flooded

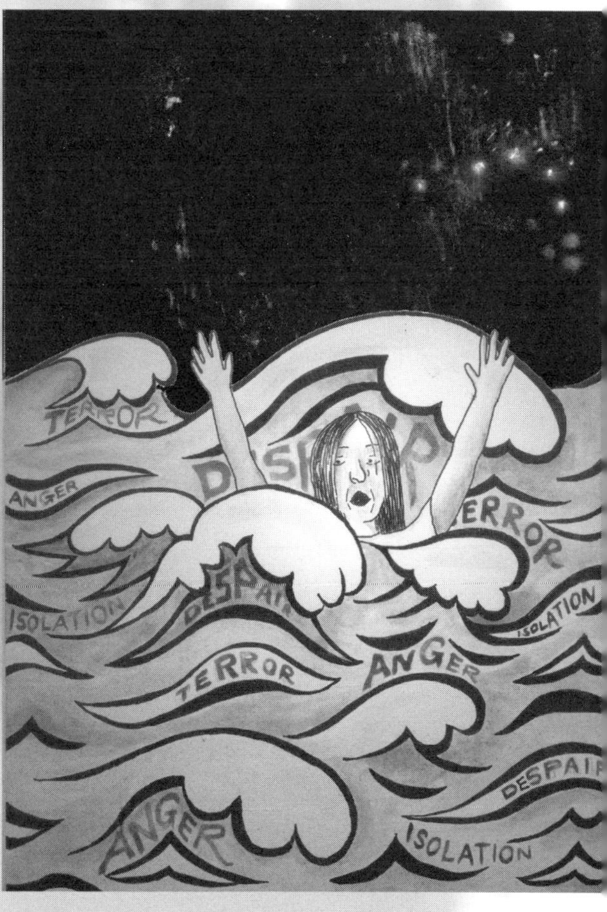
TERROR
ANGER
TERROR
DESPAIR
ISOLATION
ISOLATION
TERROR
ANGER
DESPAIR
ANGER
ISOLATION

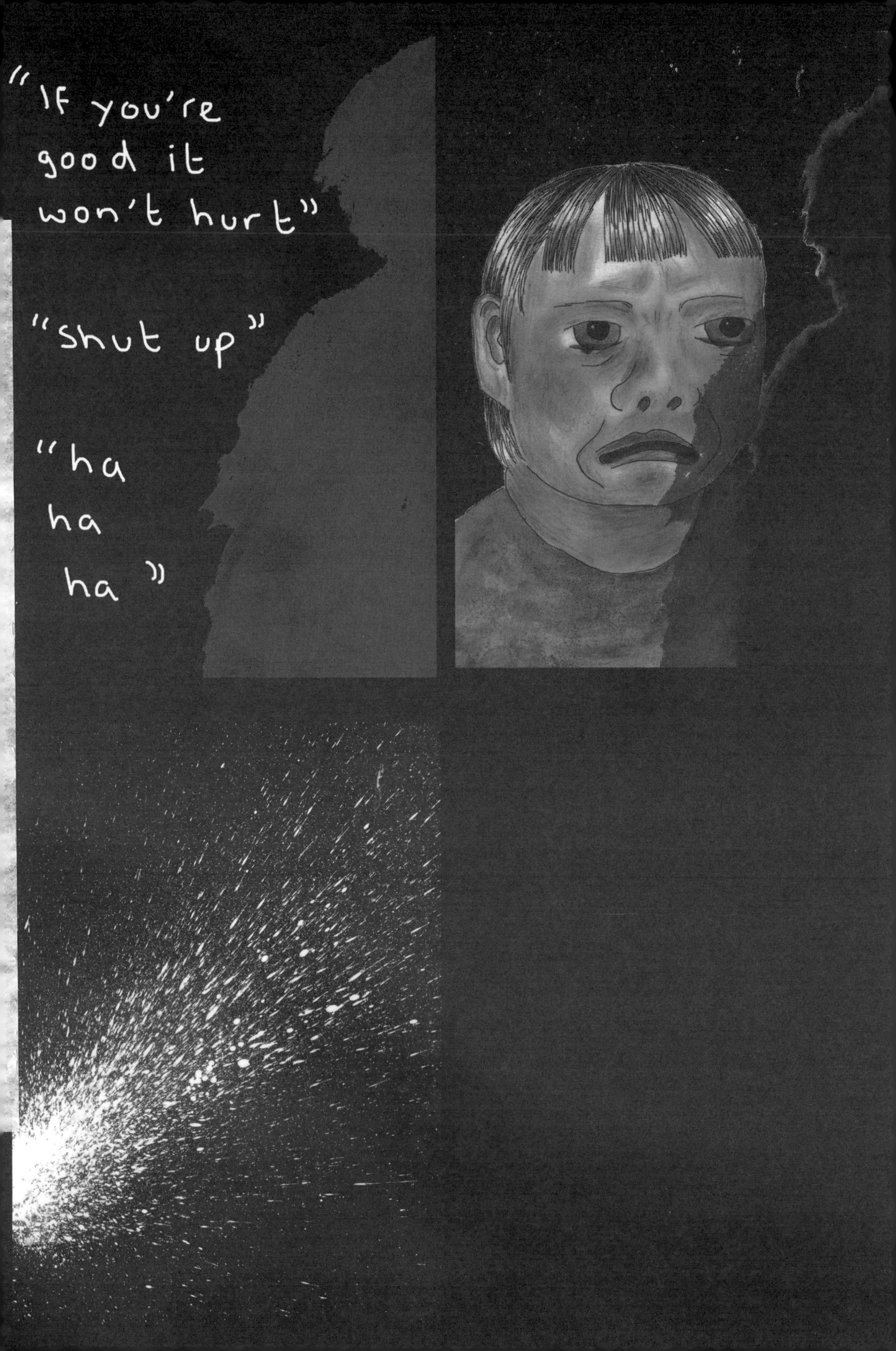
"If you're good it won't hurt"
"shut up"
"ha ha ha"

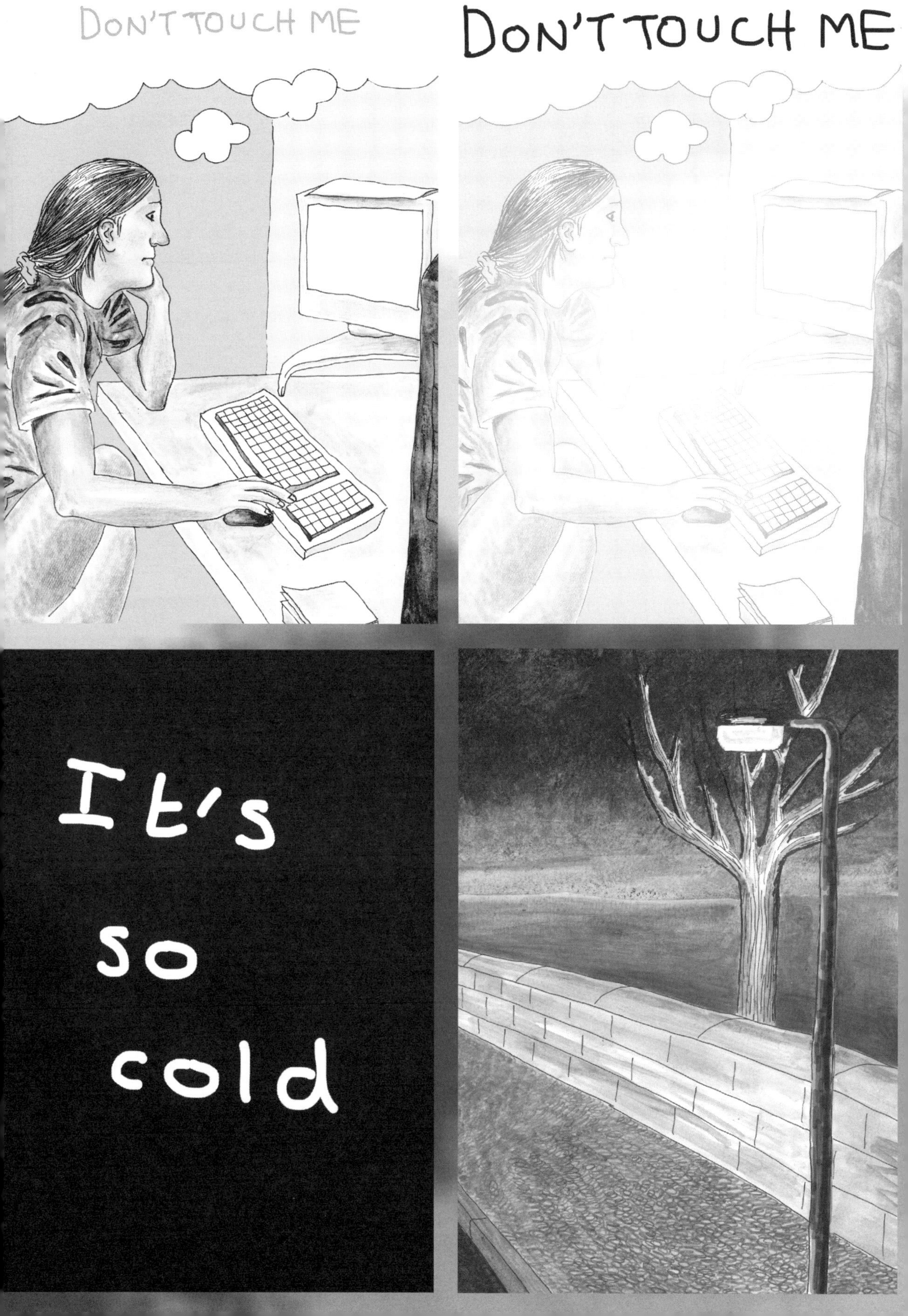
DON'T TOUCH ME
DON'T TOUCH ME
It's so cold

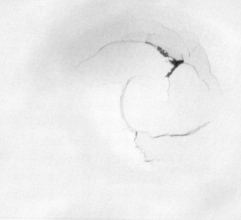

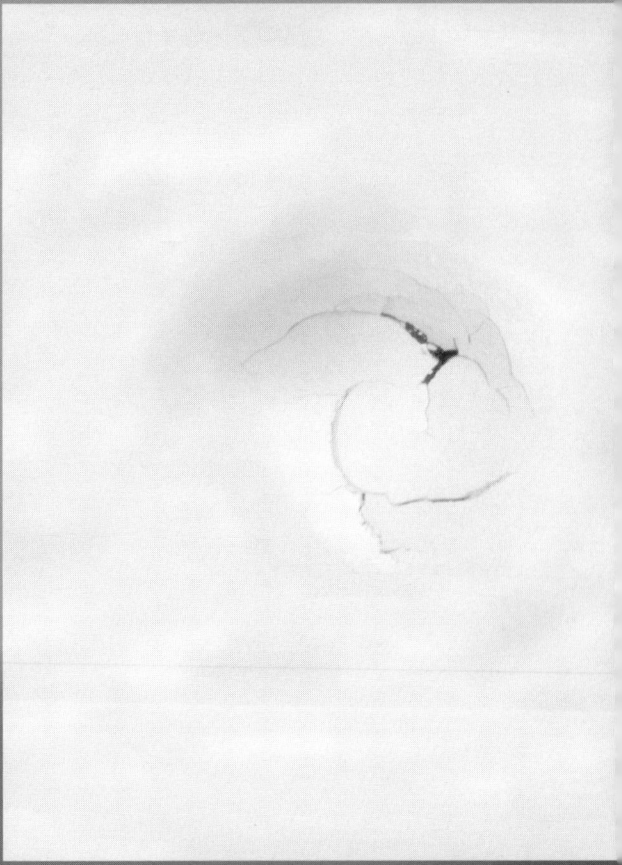

Trauma
messes
with
time

Cold

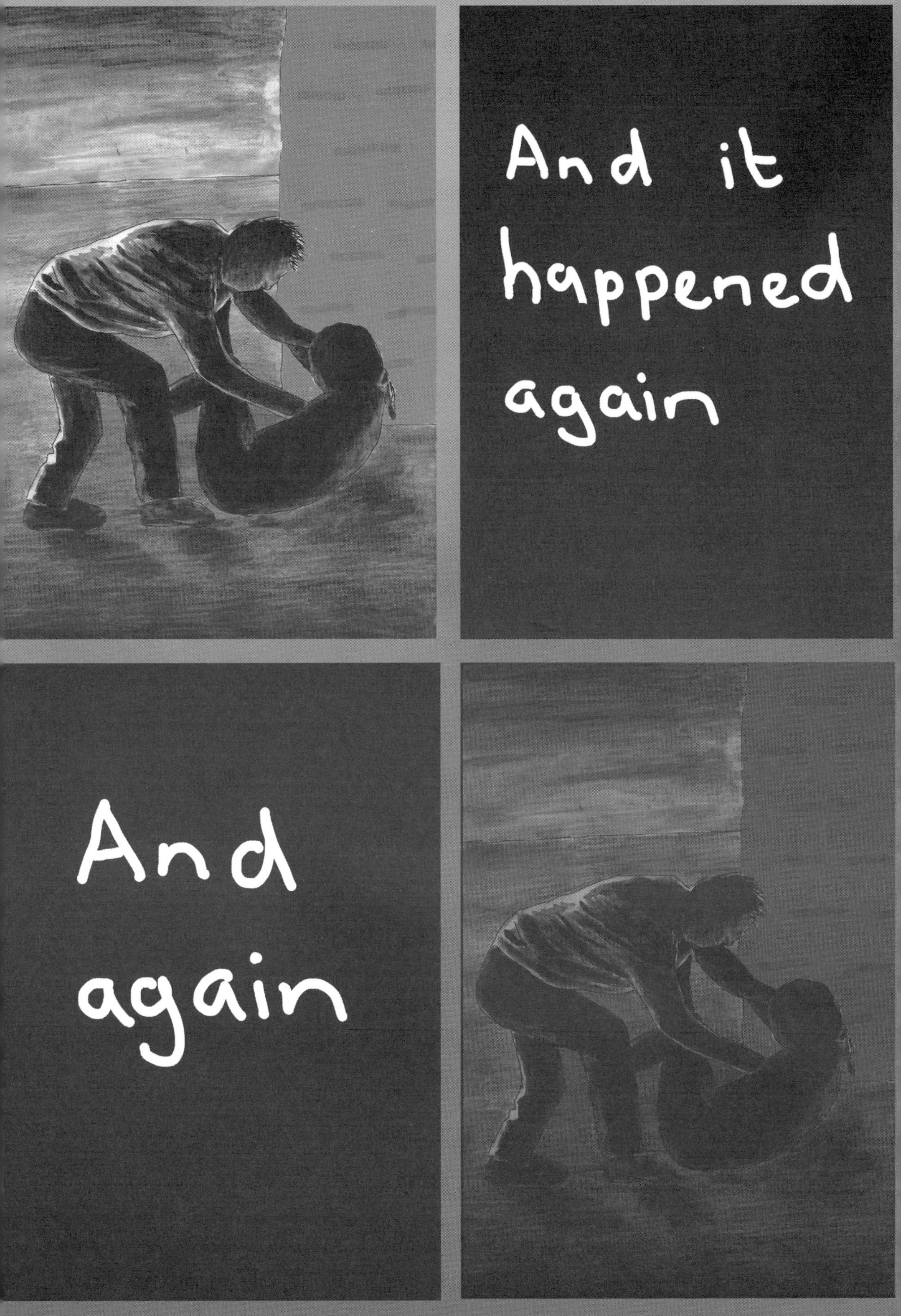
And it happened again
And again

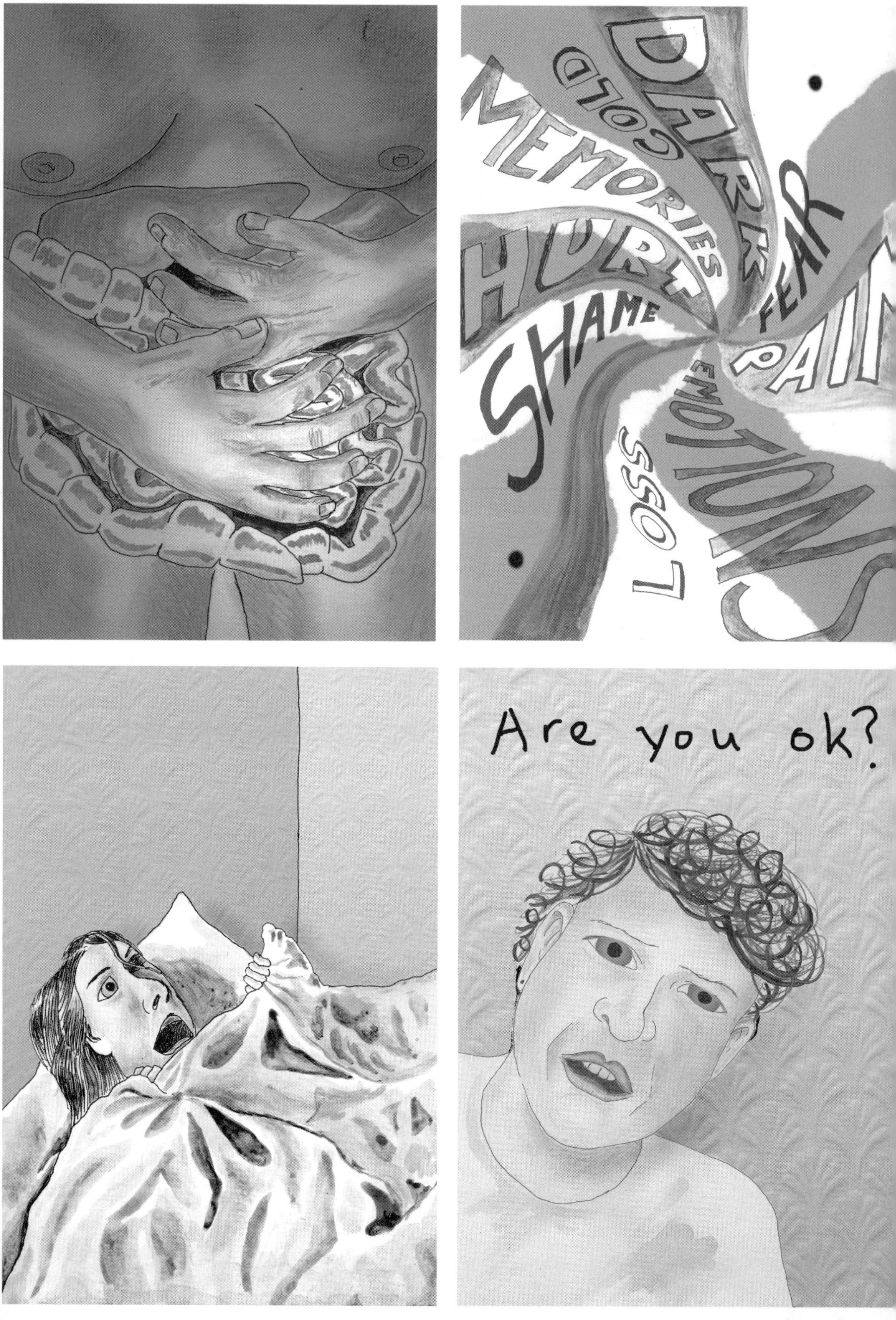
DARK
COLD
MEMORIES
HURT
SHAME
FEAR
EMOTIONS
LOSS
Are you ok?

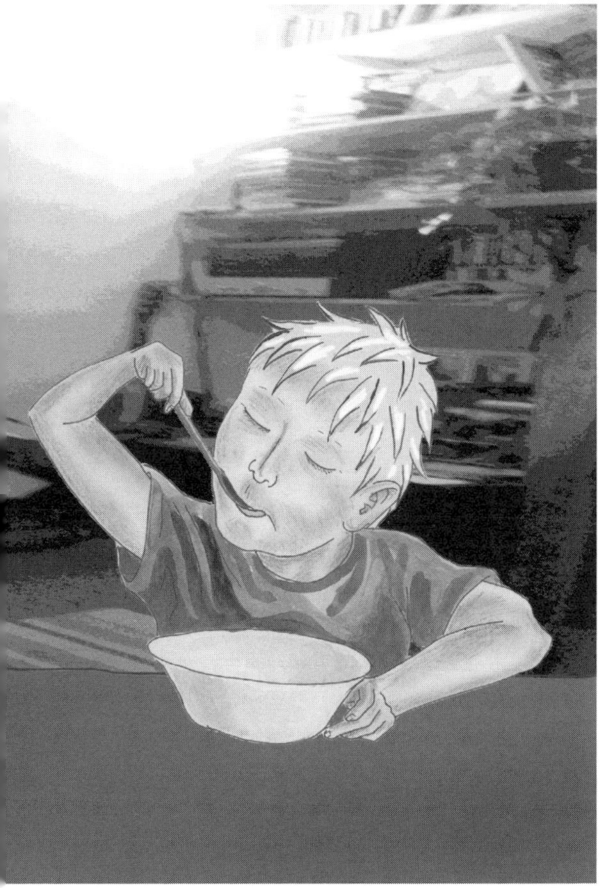

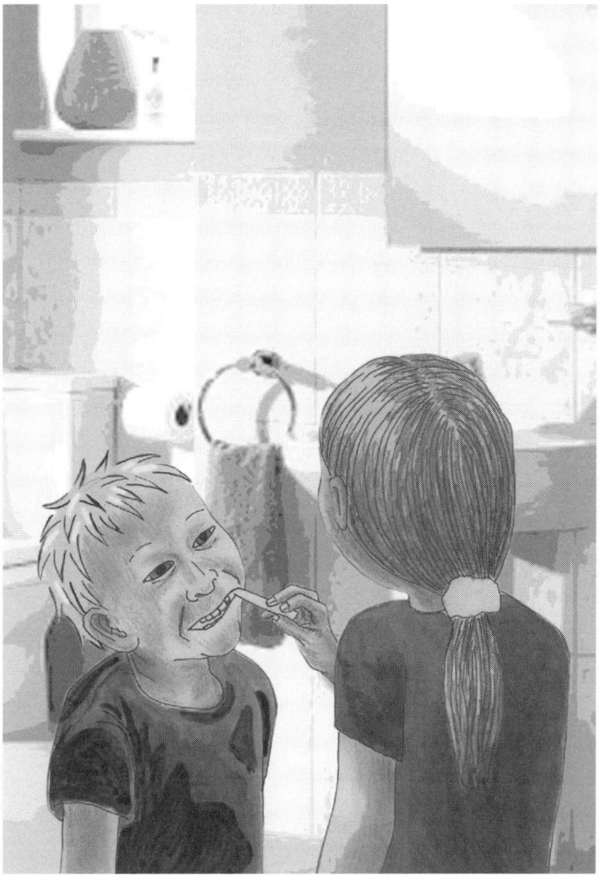

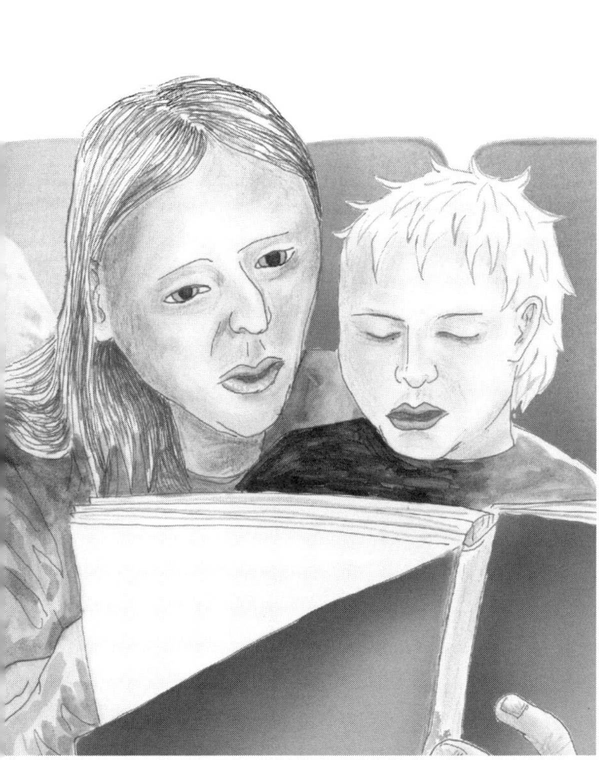

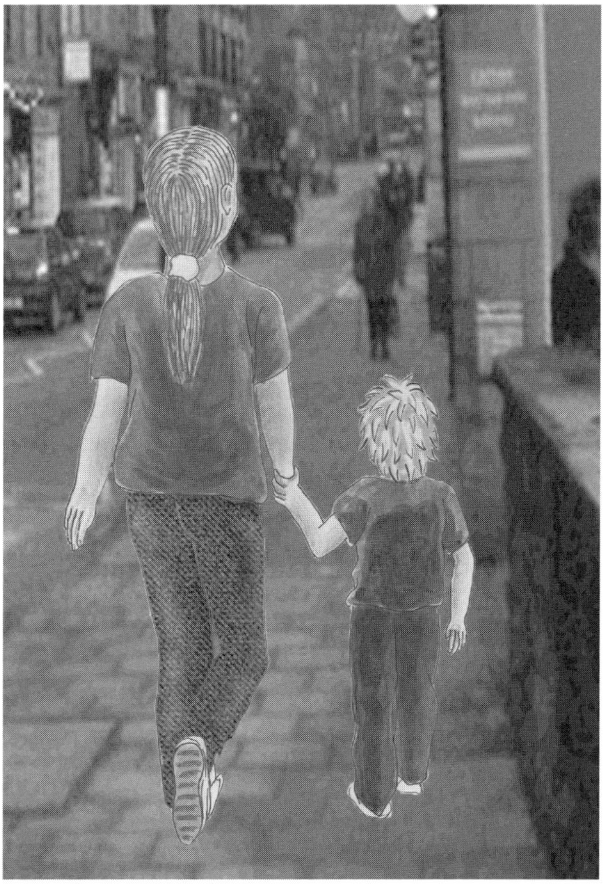

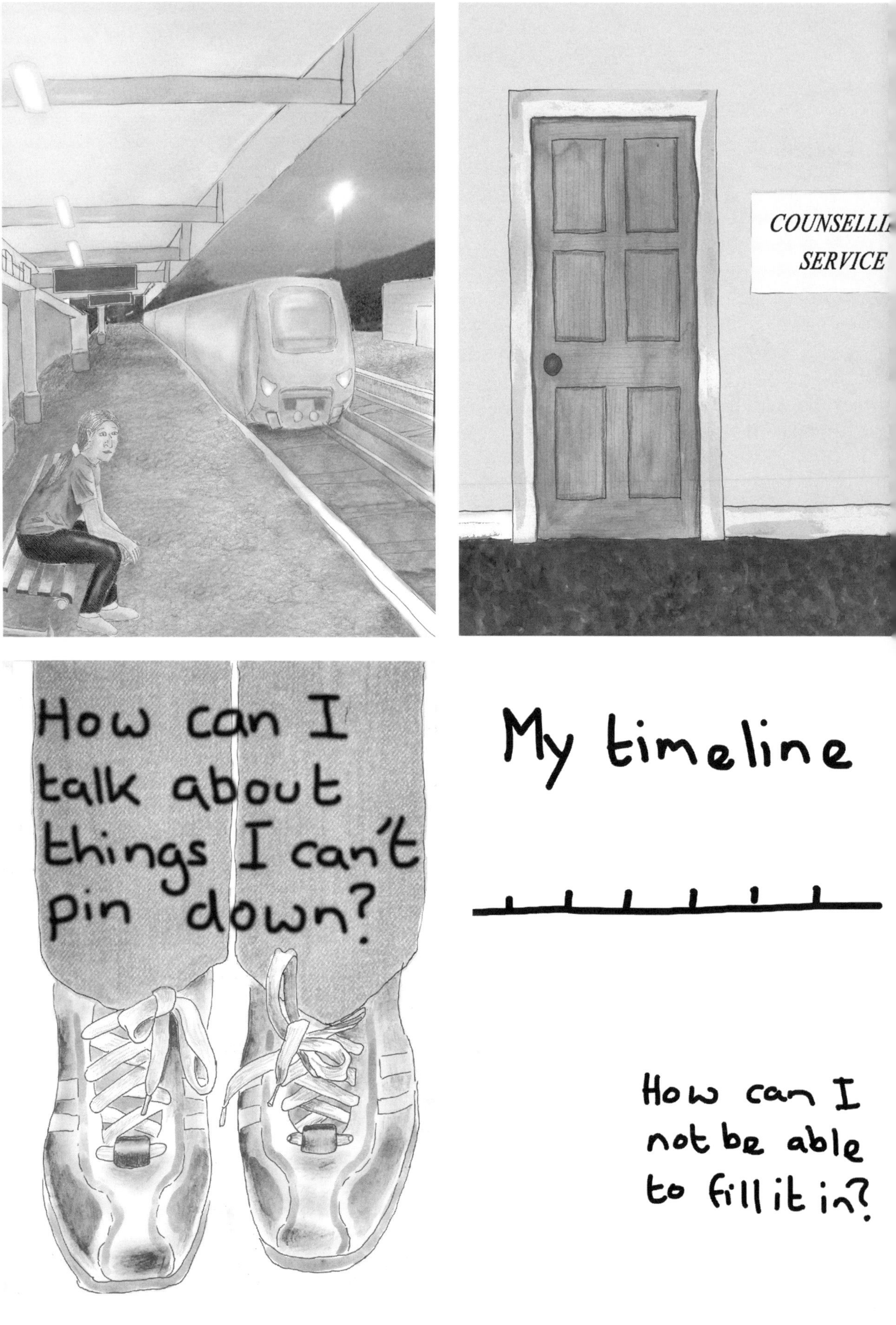
COUNSELLI
SERVICE
How can I talk about things I can't pin down?
My timeline
How can I not be able to fill it in?

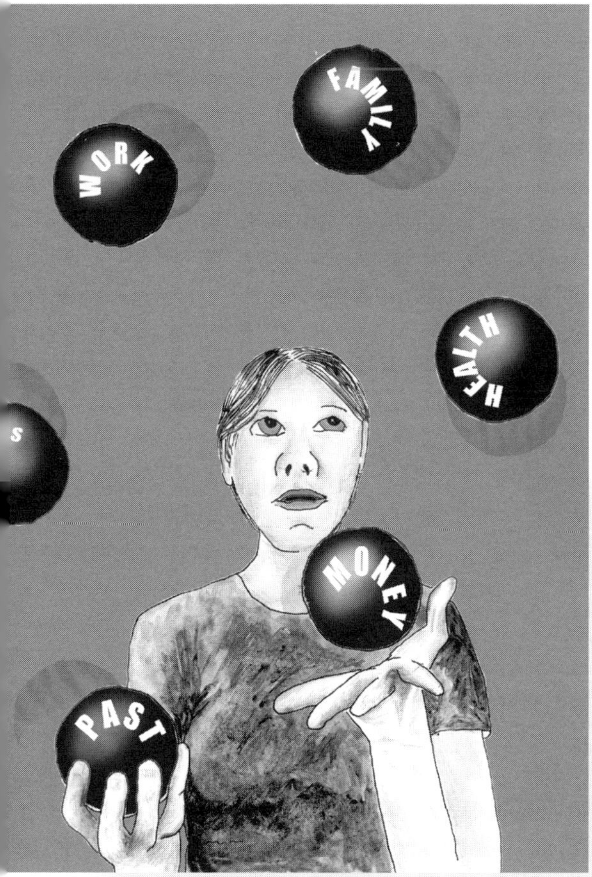
WORK
FAMILY
HEALTH
MONEY
PAST

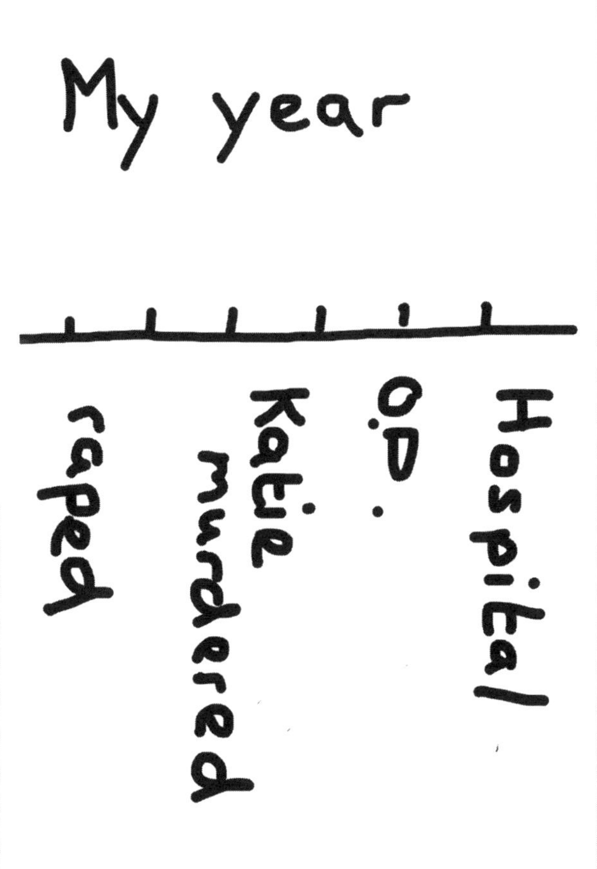
My year
raped
Katie murdered
O.D.
Hospital

It's a start.
It feels like someone else's timeline.
I don't want it to be mine

There are times to remember and times to forget

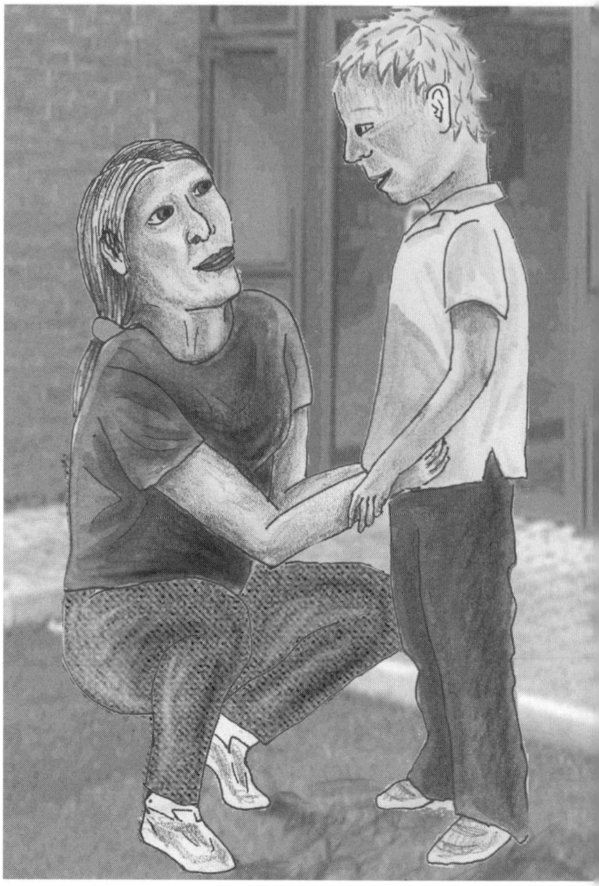

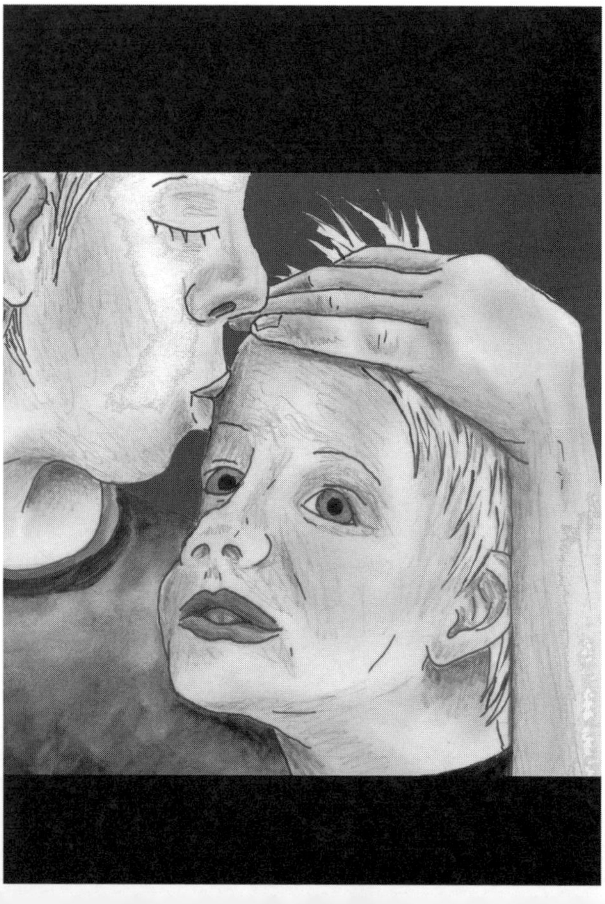

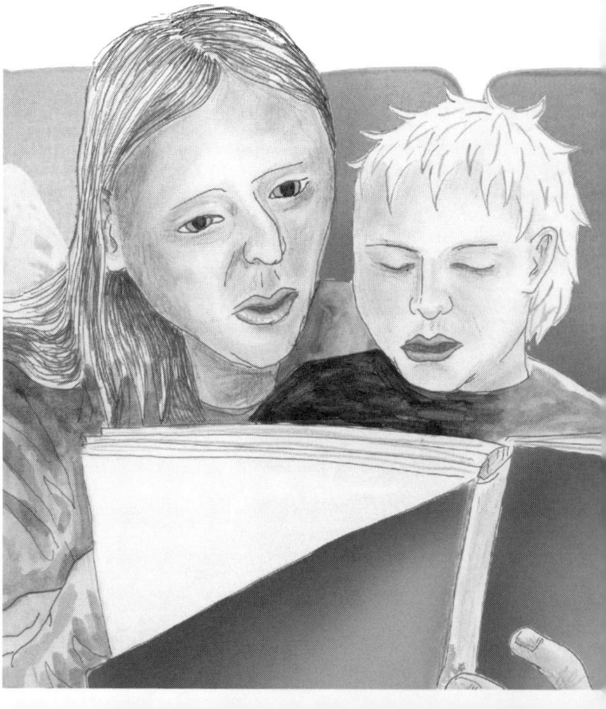

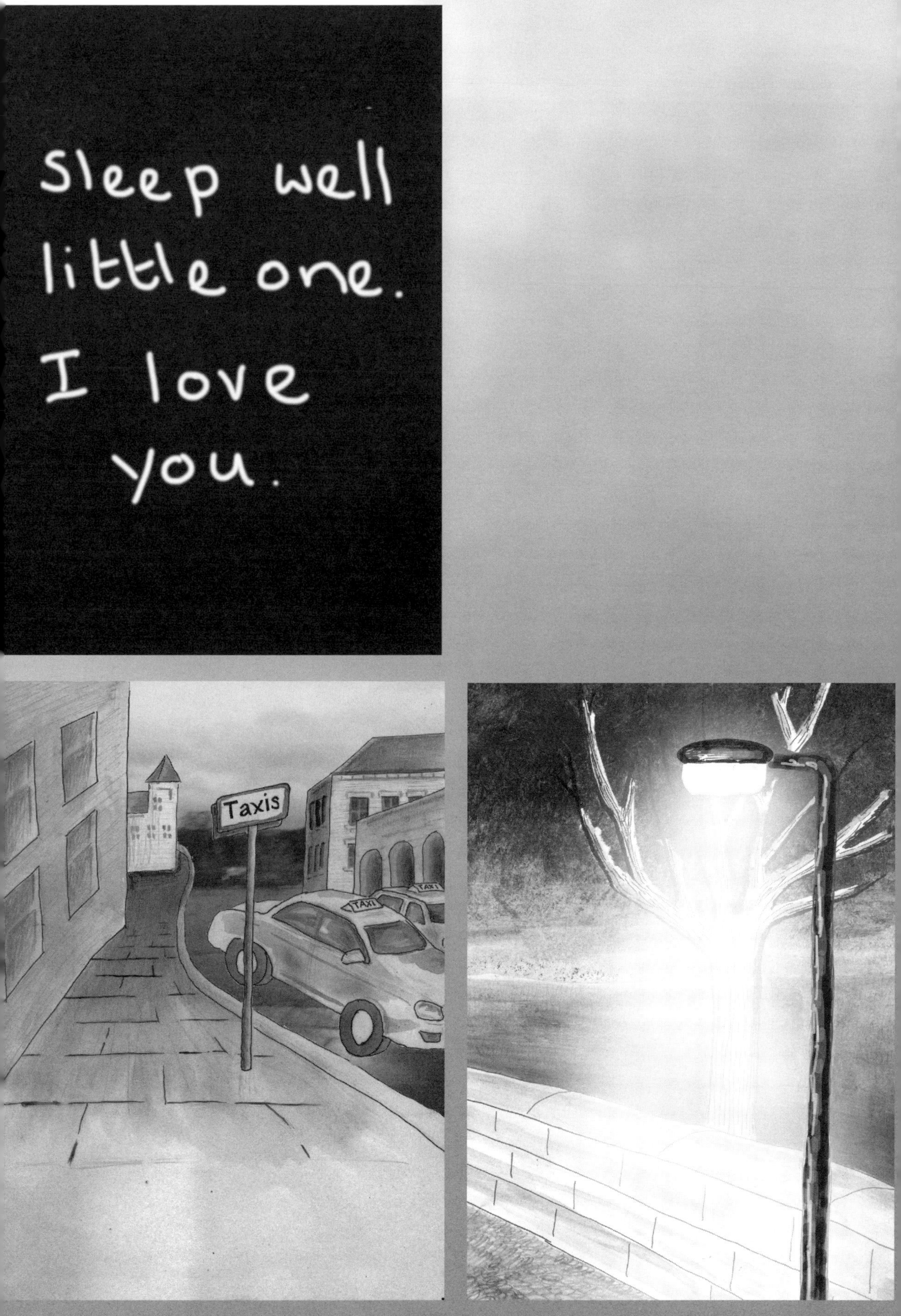
Sleep well little one. I love you.
Taxis

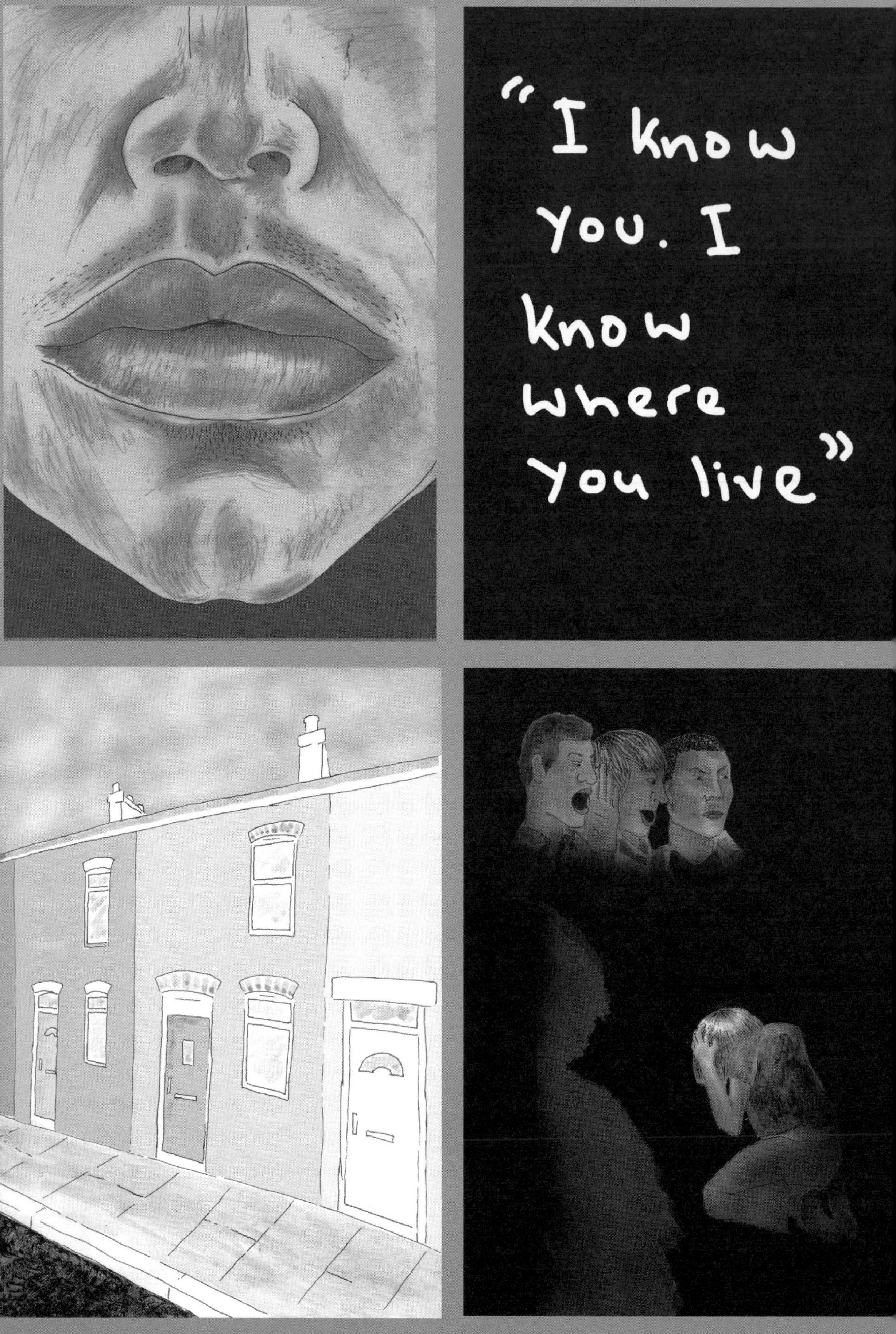
"I know you. I know where you live"

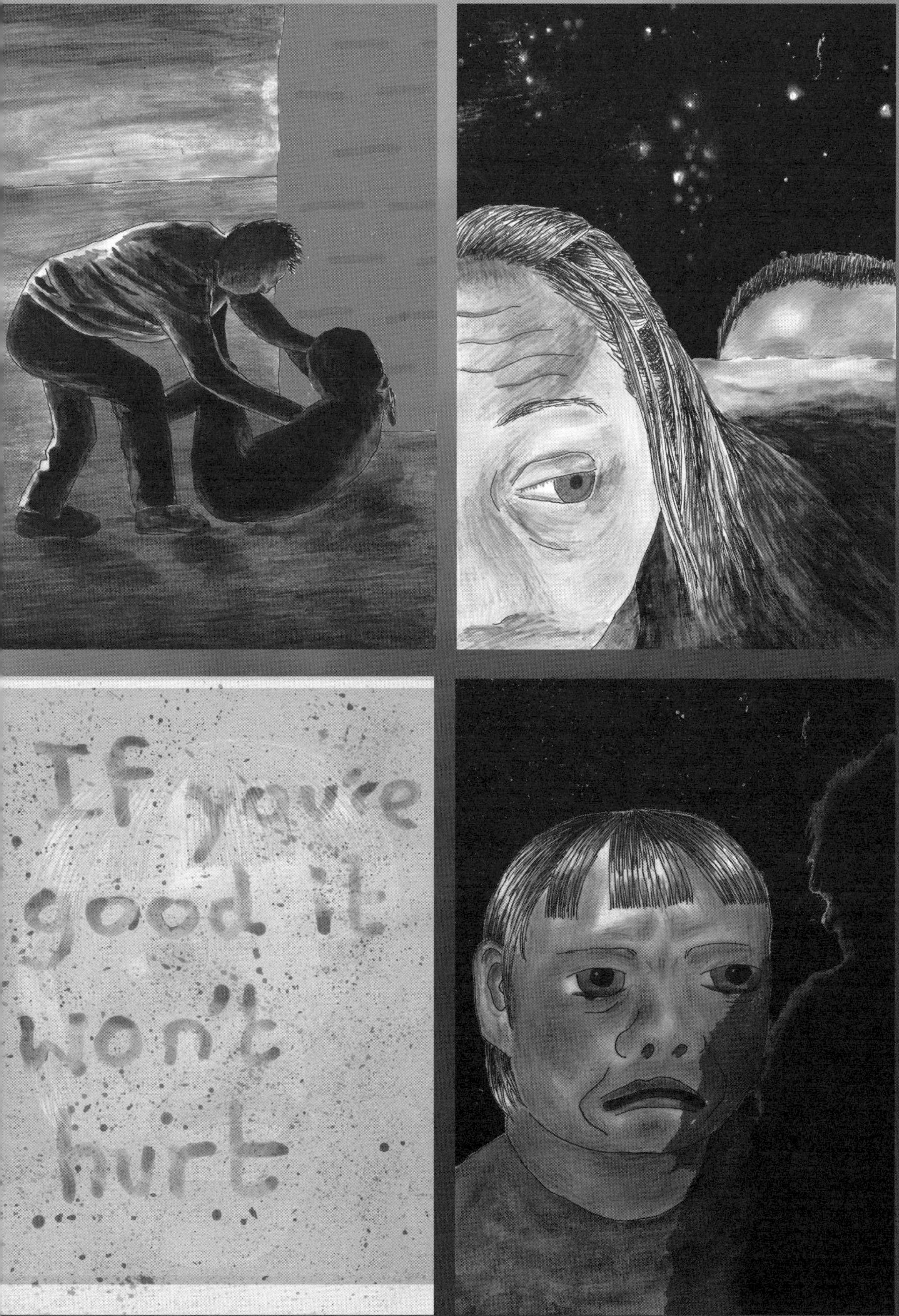
If you're
good it
won't
hurt

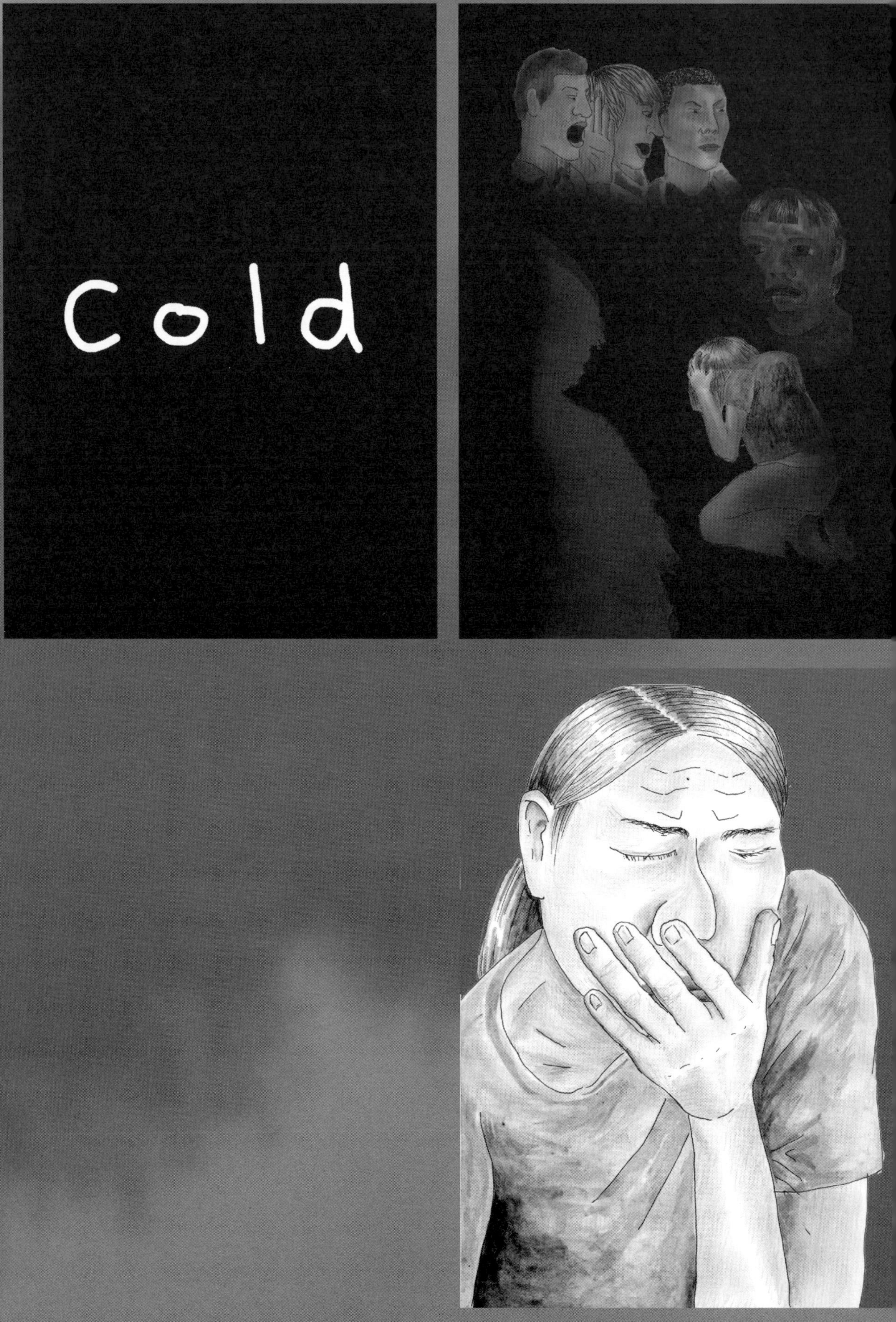
Cold

Nothing feels real anymore

Dissociation in reaction to trauma and stress. An escape when there is no escape.

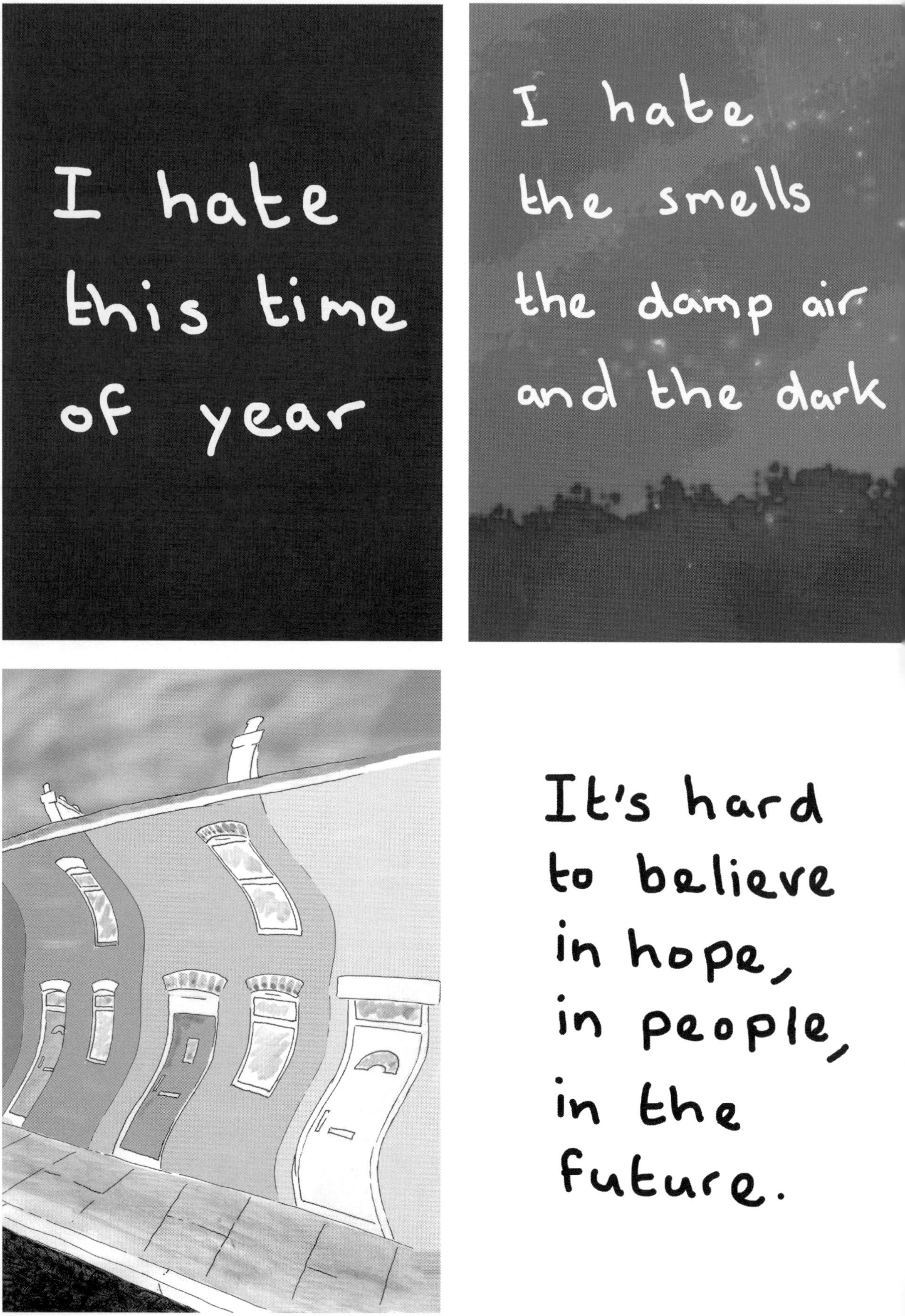
I hate this time of year
I hate the smells the damp air and the dark
It's hard to believe in hope, in people, in the future.

I can't
escape.
Nowhere
is safe.

I can't
escape.
Nowhere
is safe.

NOBODY
KNOWS
WHERE
I AM

I want
to feel
nothing

I don't want
to do this

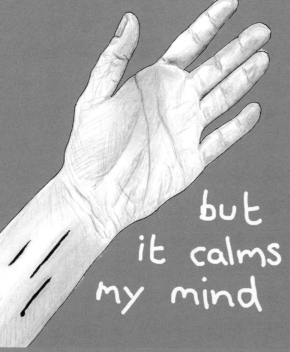

but
it calms
my mind

I wish
it would
stay
like
this

This silent
stillness
could
become
a habit

I want to escape

Drinking and self-harm provide escape

but

If we disconnect from ourselves and our experiences then we disconnect from others.

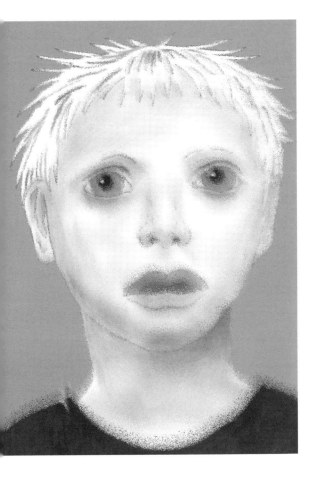

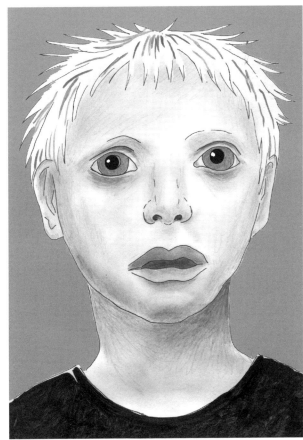

"Mummy you're not listening to me. Listen to me mummy"

I'm sorry sweetie; what were you saying?

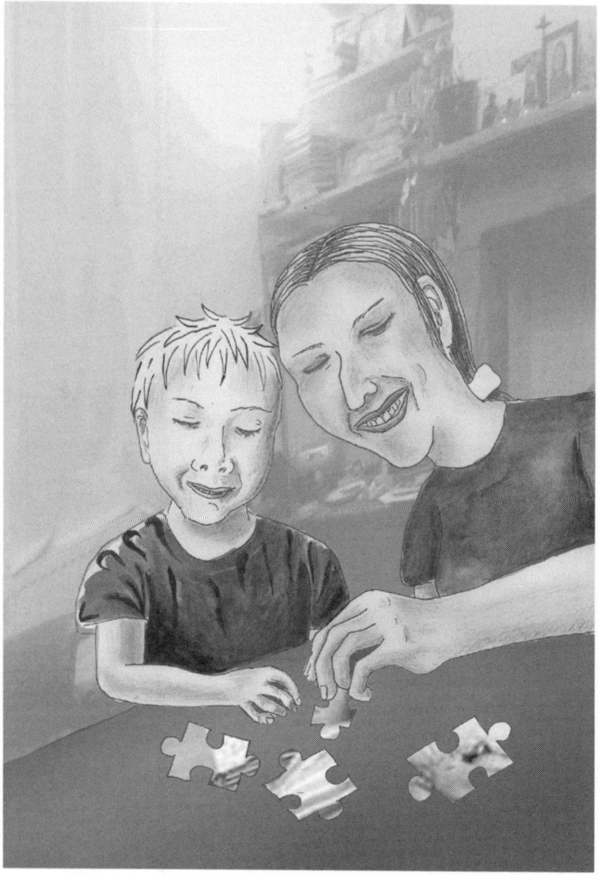

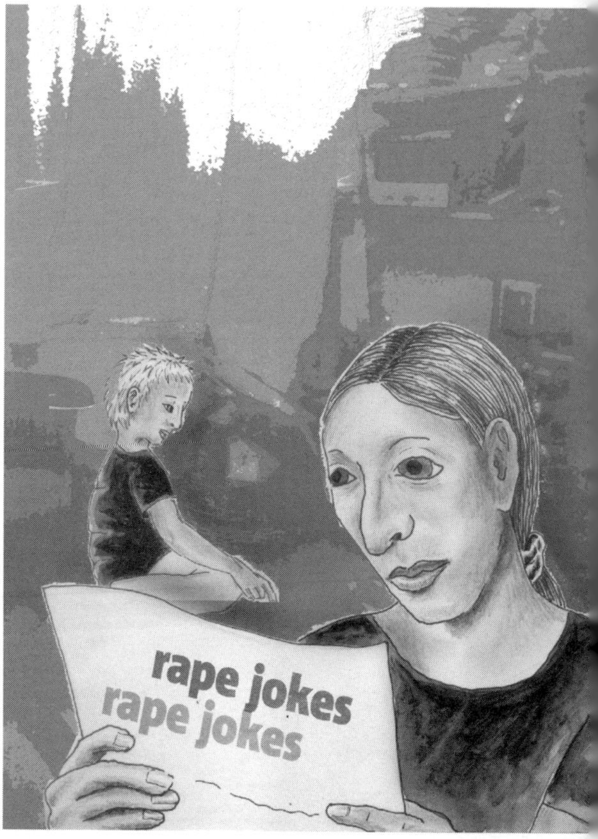
rape jokes
rape jokes

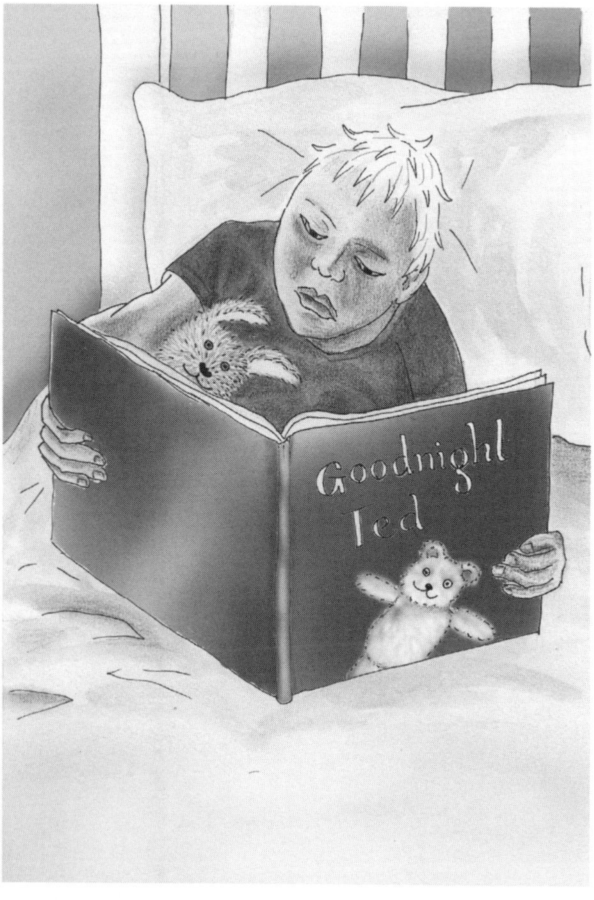
Goodnight
Ted

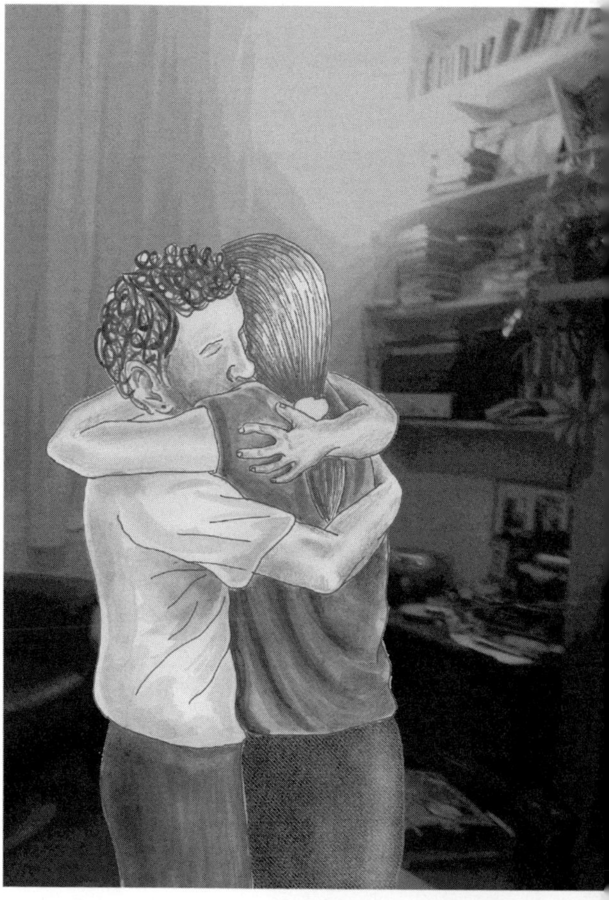

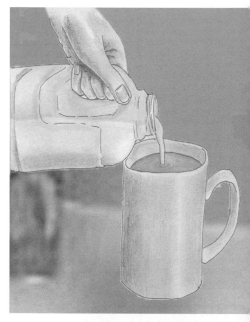

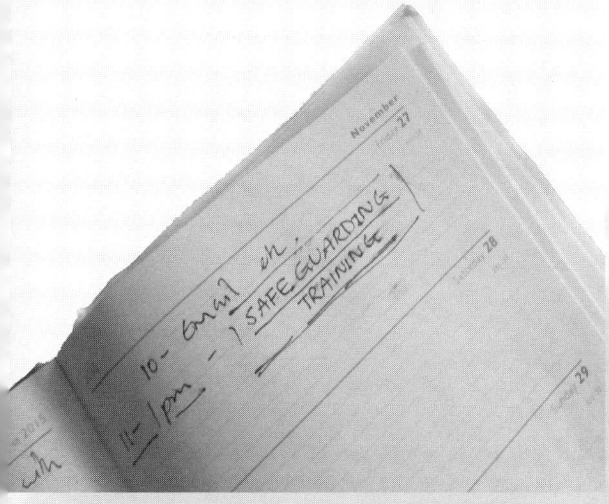
November
Friday 27
10- Email eh,
11-1pm - SAFEGUARDING
TRAINING
Saturday 28
Sunday 29

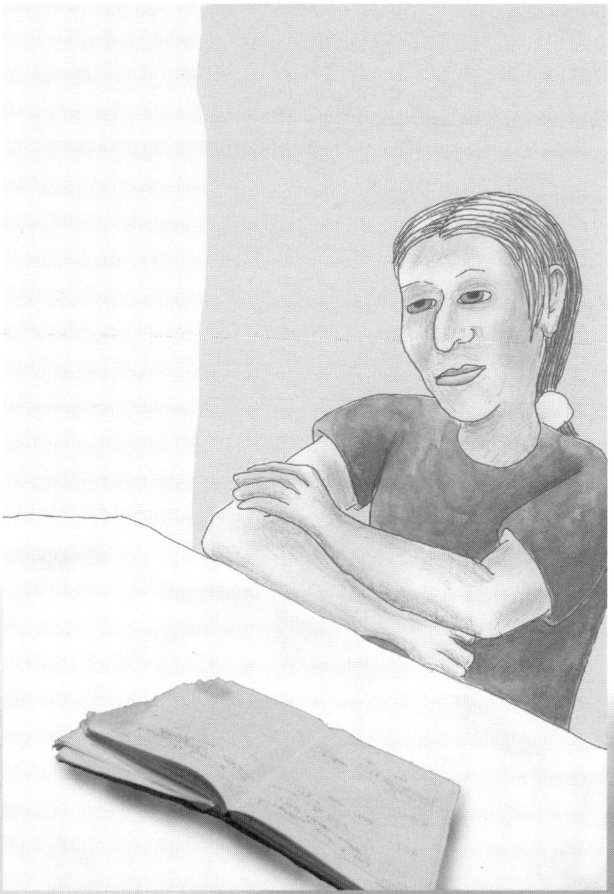

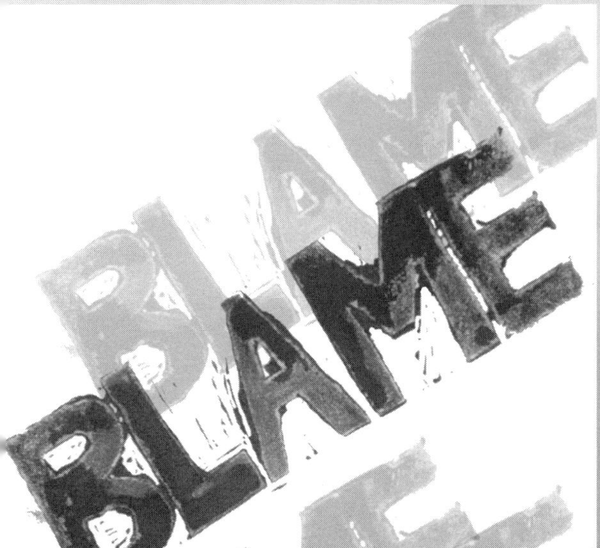
BLAME
BLAME
BLAME
BLAME

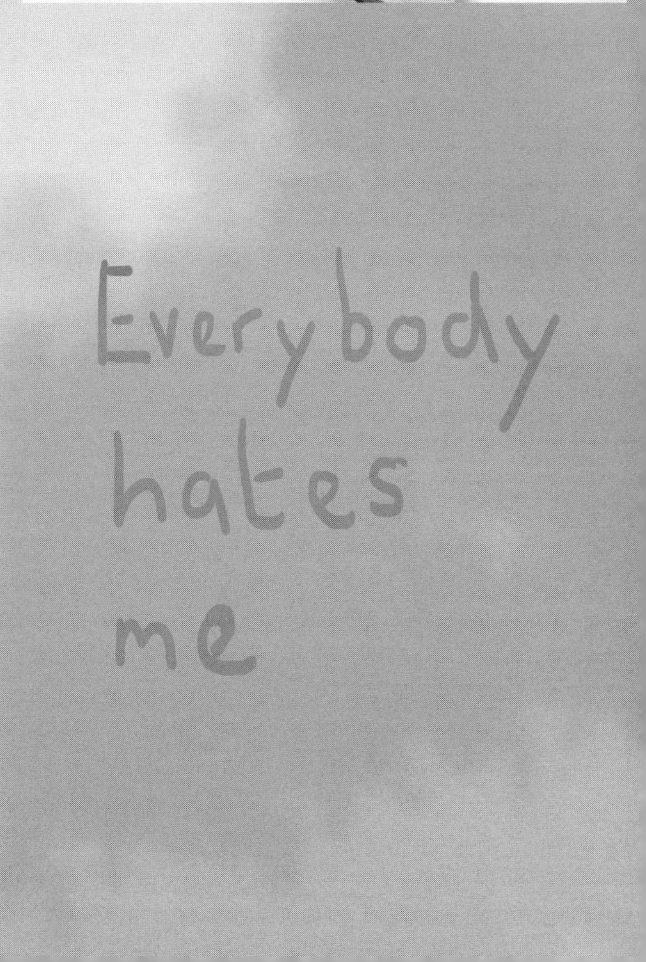
Everybody
hates
me

It's
my
fault

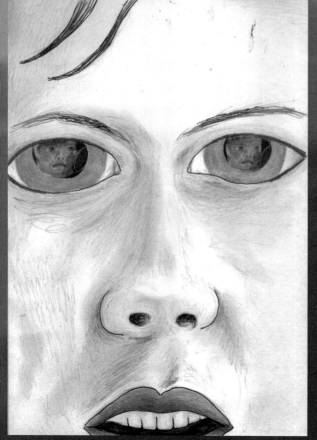

"She's
gone"

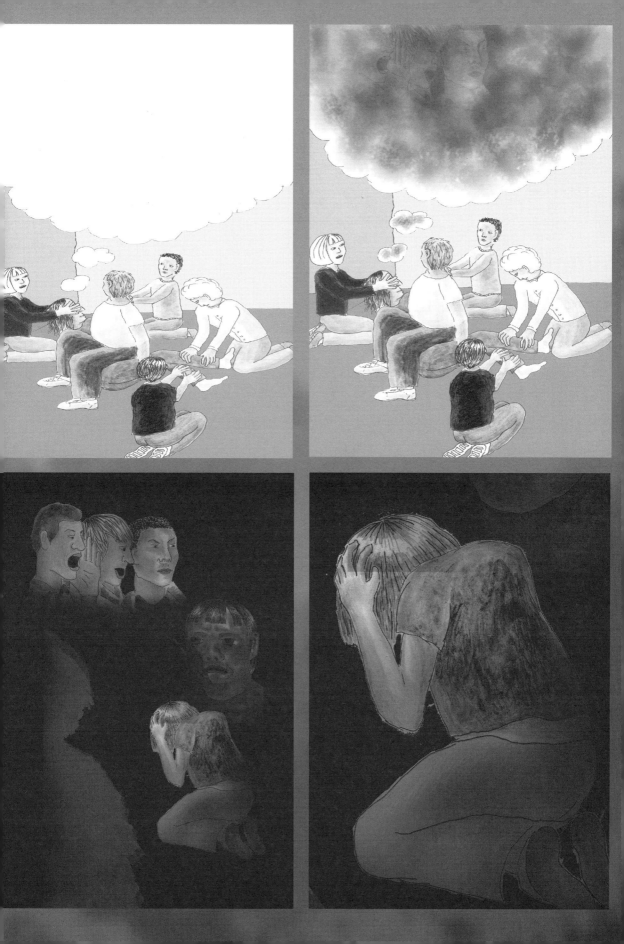

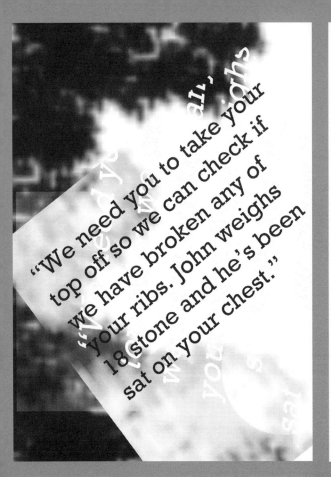

"We need you to take your top off so we can check if we have broken any of your ribs. John weighs 18 stone and he's been sat on your chest."

What a stupid way to respond to fear

It is your job to look after me. I am 15. I am not responding to you because I am lost in fear.

Physically restraining me does not help.

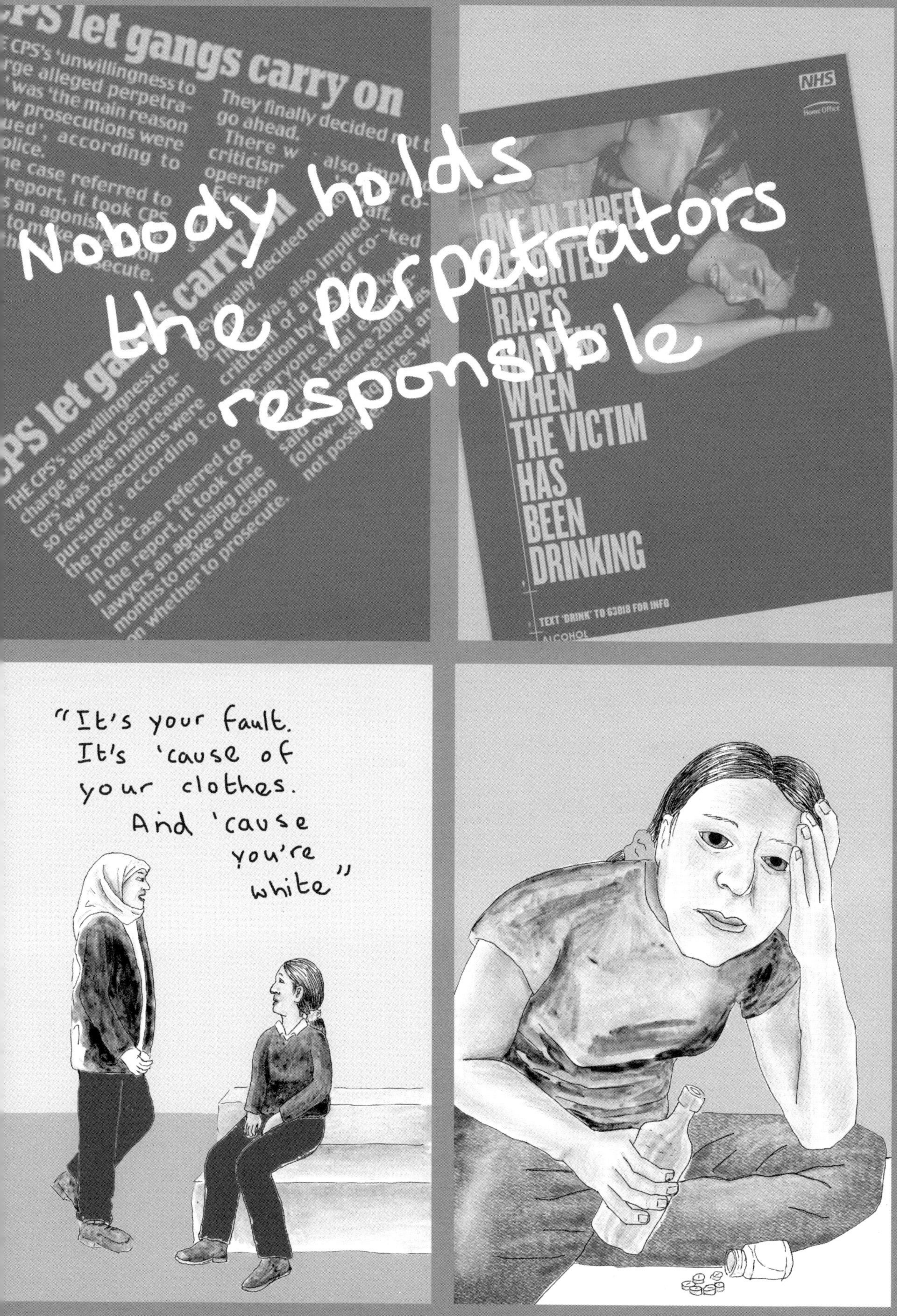
CPS let gangs carry on
THE CPS's 'unwillingness to charge alleged perpetrators' was 'the main reason so few prosecutions were pursued', according to the police.
In one case referred to in the report, it took CPS lawyers an agonising nine months to make a decision on whether to prosecute.
NHS
Home Office
ONE IN THREE REPORTED RAPES HAPPENS WHEN THE VICTIM HAS BEEN DRINKING
TEXT 'DRINK' TO 63818 FOR INFO
ALCOHOL
Nobody holds the perpetrators responsible
"It's your fault. It's 'cause of your clothes. And 'cause you're white"

... shop and she was raped by a man. ... in the evening to buy a packet of crisps from a ... West
has over-dosed on a number of occasions since. She has suffered from post-traumatic stress since and
Hospital on a regular basis for the past two years. She has been seeing Dr H...
your life and caused a great deal of turmoil in your li... You told me h...

The police have told you you c...
Since I have discovered that the ...
new form and I have now comple...
quick read of this application and ...
to sign too, which would therefor...
investigtions with the police, med...
to ask her to read through the a...

... you could provide me ...
... understand ...
Adolesence psyc...

We understand fro...
regard to the incid...
took place.

We would ask you to ...
indicates that [redacted] w...
has further indicated that ...
years. The report does inc...
Dr [redacted] clearly states ...
dealing with that has clearl...

You have also requested a rep... ...on
report of 15 April 1997, it is cl... ...t two
in December 1994, October 19... ...l incident.
place after the reported sexual assault. Indeed, ... she has been
thinks she is likely to continue episodes of self-harm. ...rapy.

...ate that at paragraph 3 of his
...as admitted to [redacted] for overdoses
...ary 1997. All these incidents took
[redacted] indicates at paragraph 4 that he

C...

Regis...

F...
P...

Printed by [redacted] (Admin/Clinical Support Access Role)

3 of 3

Summary

CS = Chronic Summary MS = Major Summary OS = Minor Summary S = Unsp...
OE = Ongoing Episode

Aug 1994	Self-injurious behaviour (X766K)
	MULTIPLE LACERATIONS ARMS
Dec 1994	[X]Sexual assault by bodily force (U3L..)
Dec 1994	Drug overdose (Xa4eX)
Oct 1995	Drug overdose (Xa4eX)
May 1996	Drug overdose (Xa4eX)
Oct 1996	Migraine (F26..)
Nov 1996	Drug overdose (Xa4eX)
Feb 1997	Drug overdose (Xa4eX)
Oct 2002	[X]Depressive episode, unspecified (XE1Zb)
Mar 2003	Drug overdose (Xa4eX)

Pathology Results

No information recorded

Active Problems

No information recorded

A QUALITY SERV...
Approved by The Legal Aid B...

...a...

...y of current illn...

...appreciate an assessme... [redacted] on 28.10.02...
...e from [redacted]

...first came into contact with child a...
...ars old, when she began to self-harm. ...
...erself with a razor. This continued and at 15 ...
...itted to [redacted] Hospital. This is the only prev...
...a Mental Health Hospital.

...istrict Care Trust working in partnership with the [redacted] Council

Chairman...
Chief Execu...

Legal Aid

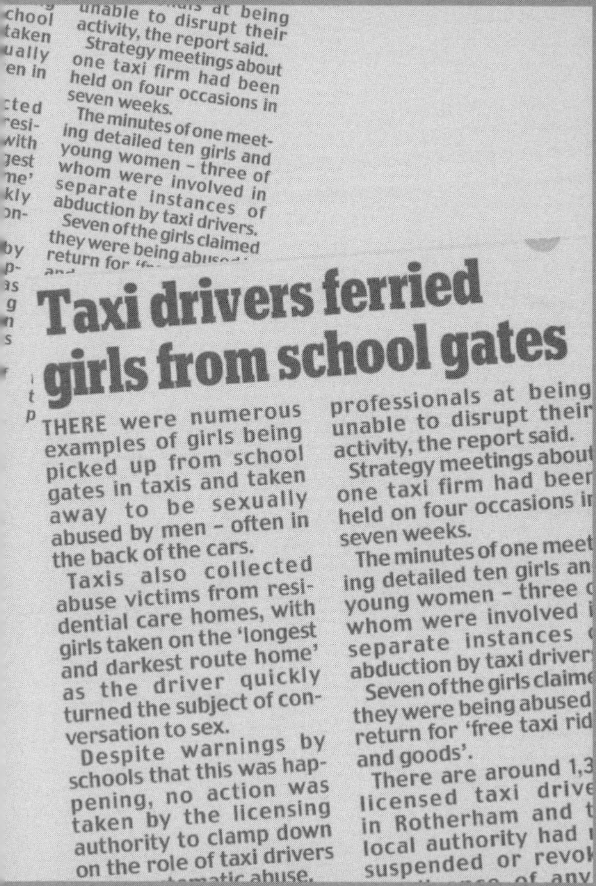

...unable to disrupt their activity, the report said.
Strategy meetings about one taxi firm had been held on four occasions in seven weeks.
The minutes of one meeting detailed ten girls and young women – three of whom were involved in separate instances of abduction by taxi drivers.
Seven of the girls claimed they were being abused in return for...

Taxi drivers ferried girls from school gates

THERE were numerous examples of girls being picked up from school gates in taxis and taken away to be sexually abused by men – often in the back of the cars.

Taxis also collected abuse victims from residential care homes, with girls taken on the 'longest and darkest route home' as the driver quickly turned the subject of conversation to sex.

Despite warnings by schools that this was happening, no action was taken by the licensing authority to clamp down on the role of taxi drivers on the ...tematic abuse.

professionals at being unable to disrupt their activity, the report said.

Strategy meetings about one taxi firm had been held on four occasions in seven weeks.

The minutes of one meet... ing detailed ten girls an... young women – three ... whom were involved i... separate instances ... abduction by taxi driver...

Seven of the girls claime... they were being abused ... return for 'free taxi rid... and goods'.

There are around 1,3... licensed taxi drive... in Rotherham and t... local authority had ... suspended or revok...

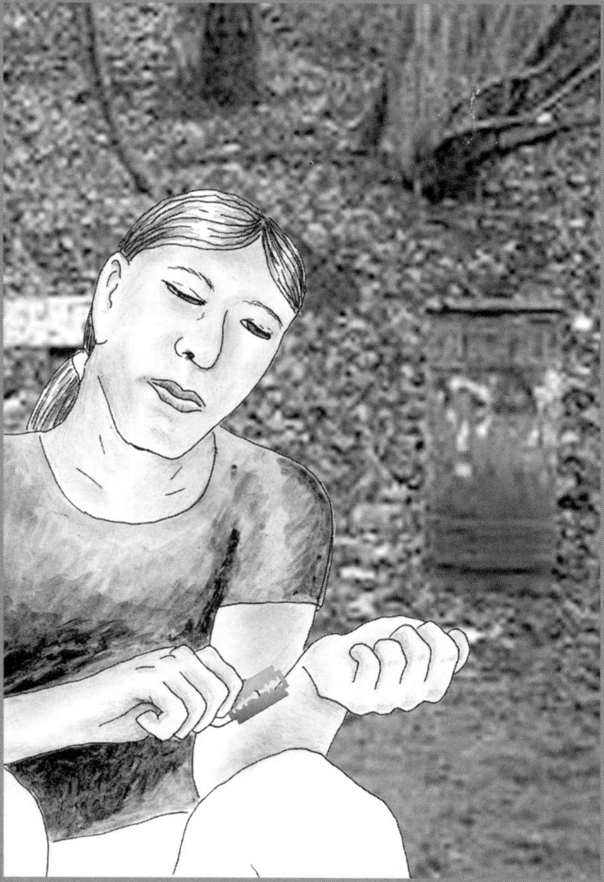

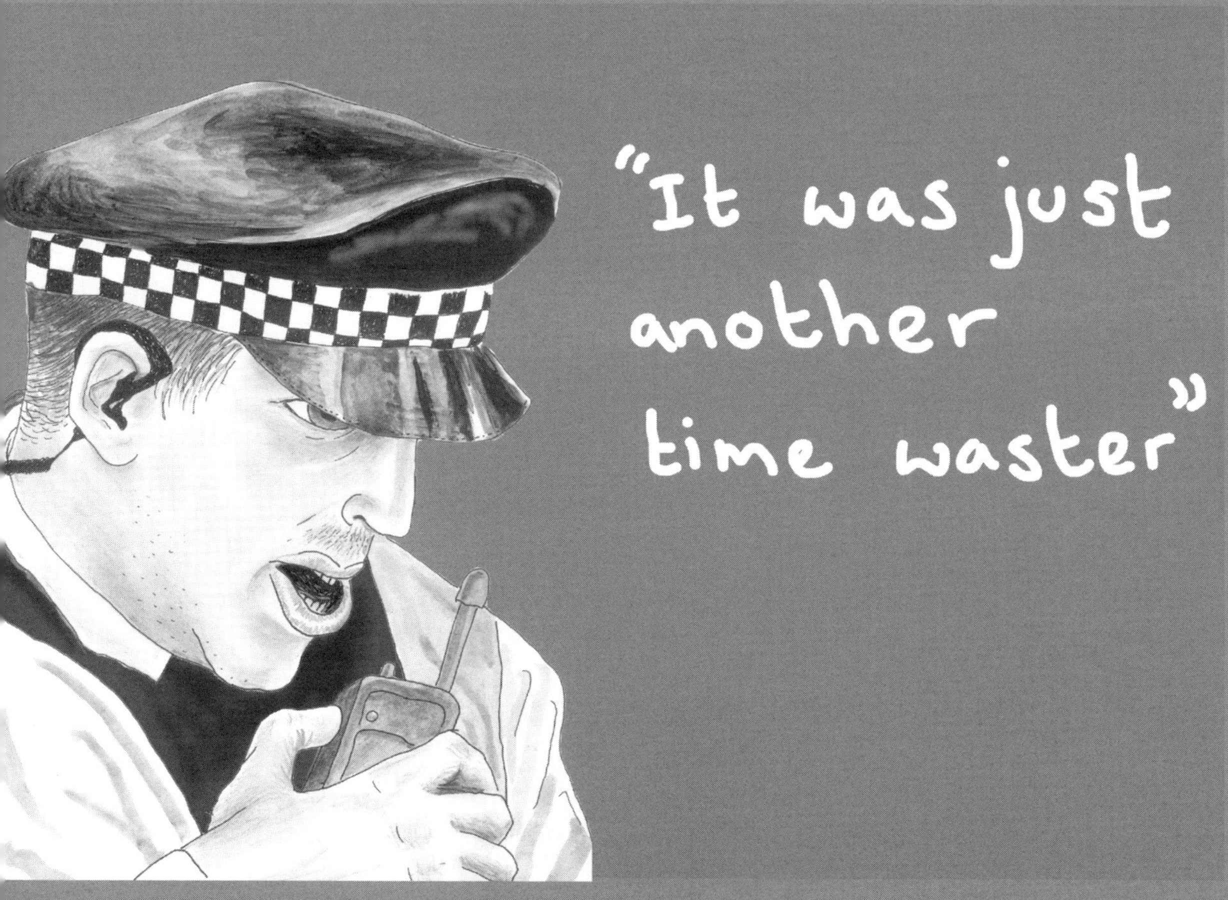
"It was just another time waster"

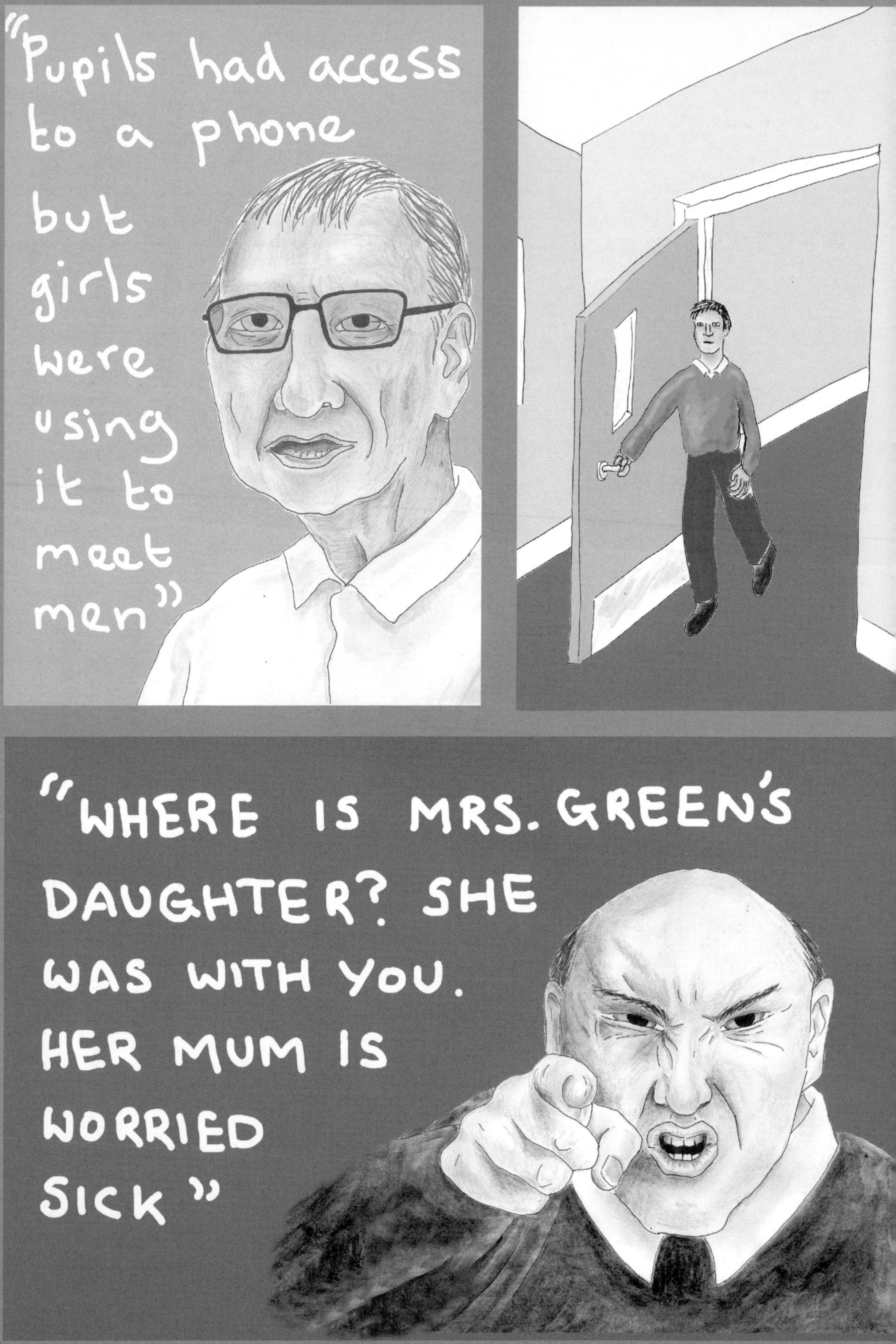
"Pupils had access to a phone but girls were using it to meet men"
"WHERE IS MRS. GREEN'S DAUGHTER? SHE WAS WITH YOU. HER MUM IS WORRIED SICK"

Mrs. Green's boyfriend abuses her daughter. Why does she care if someone else is doing that too?

Maybe they think it's worse being raped by an asian man?

But I don't say that; I just think it.

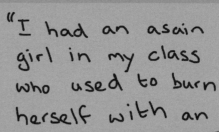

"I had an asain girl in my class who used to burn herself with an iron"

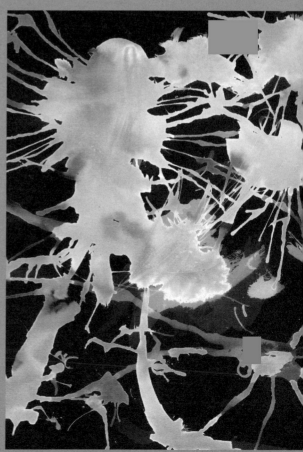

"Her uncle was abusing her. It was hard for her to tell anyone."

- 31% of young women aged 18–24 report having experienced sexual abuse in childhood (NSPCC 2011).

- Only around 15% of those who experience sexual violence choose to report to the police.

- Approximately 90% of those who are raped know the perpetrator prior to the offence (Ministry of Justice, ONS and Home Office 2013).

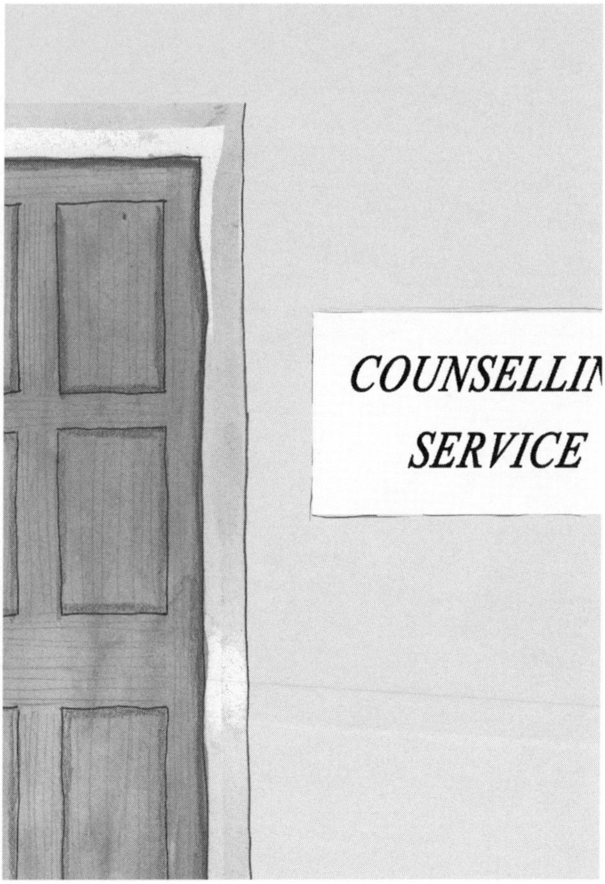
COUNSELLIN
SERVICE

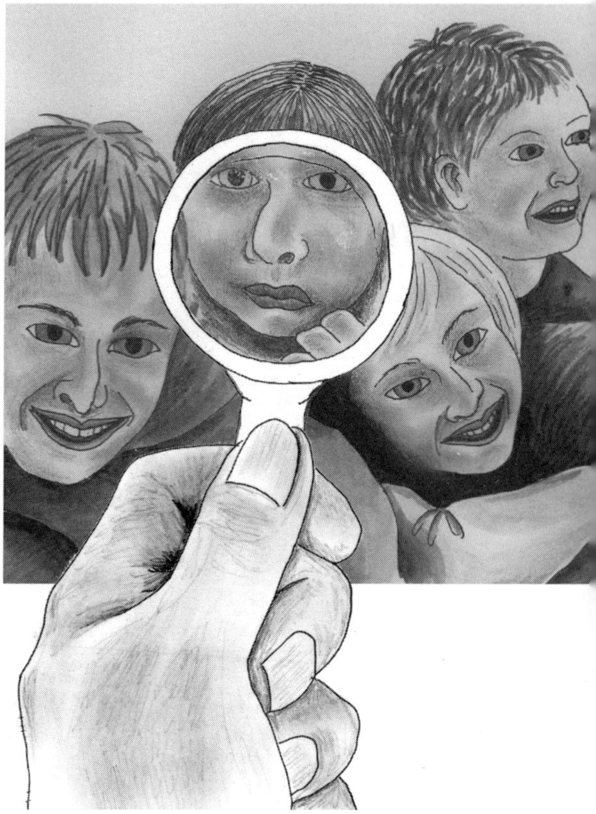

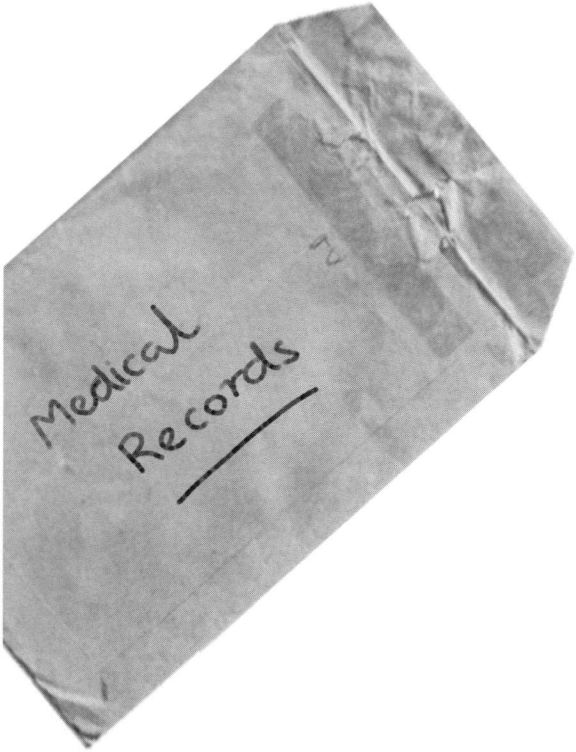
Medical
Records

"What would
you do
if you were
supporting
yourself when
you were
younger?"

I wouldn't have done what they did.

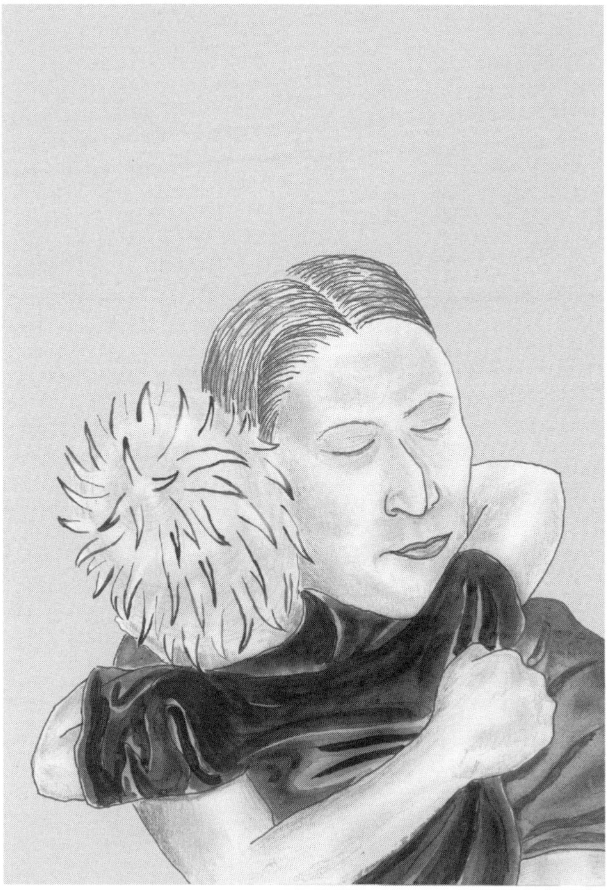

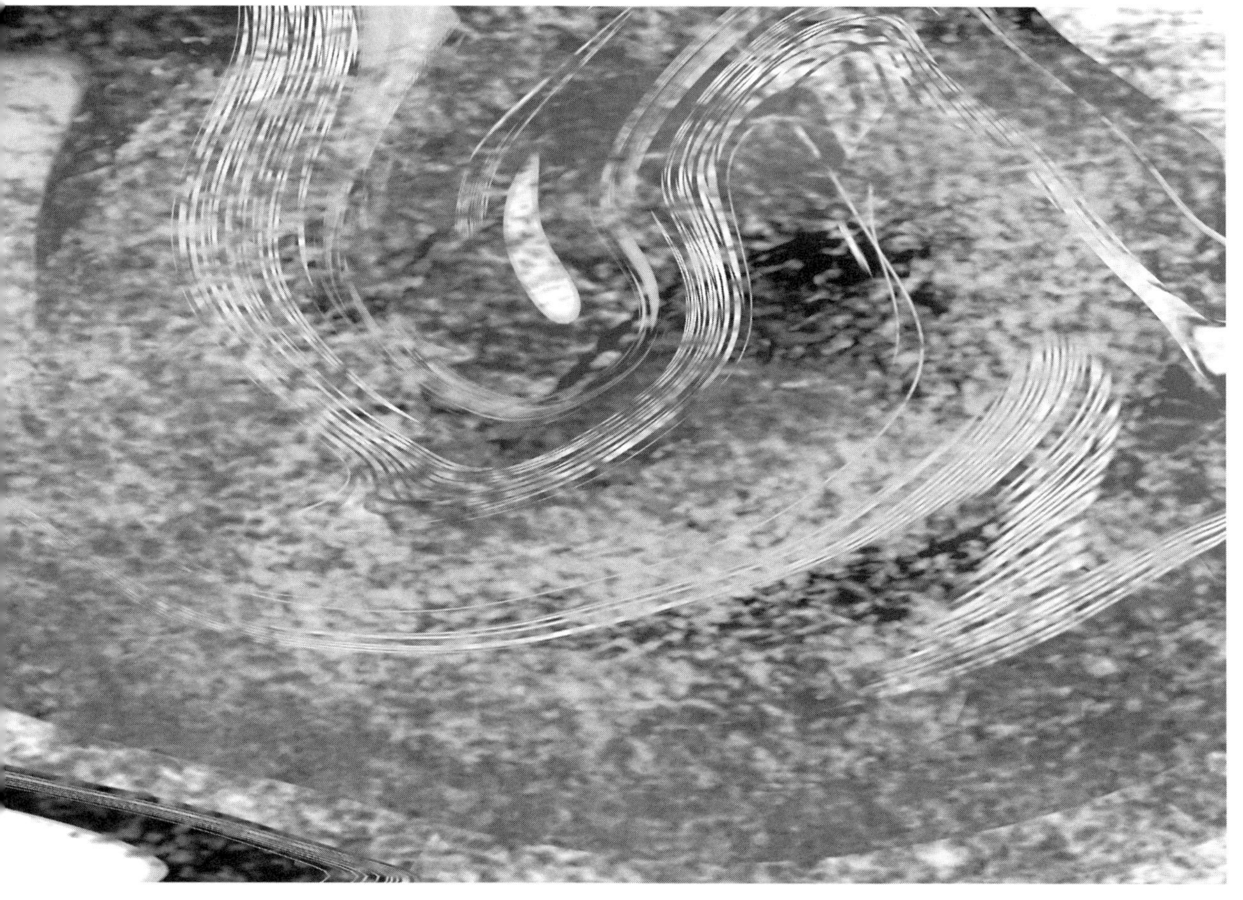

How did
this happen
to me?

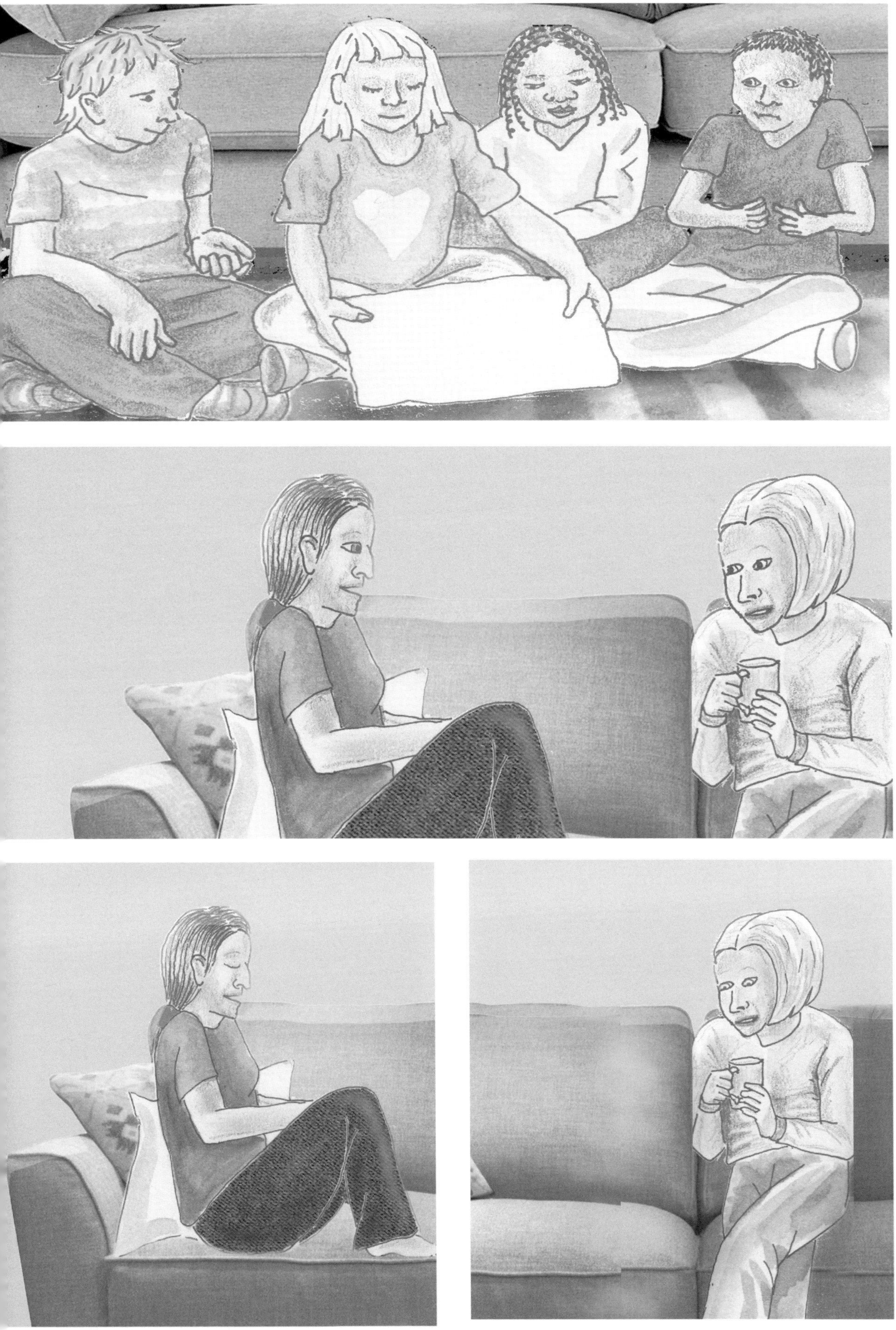

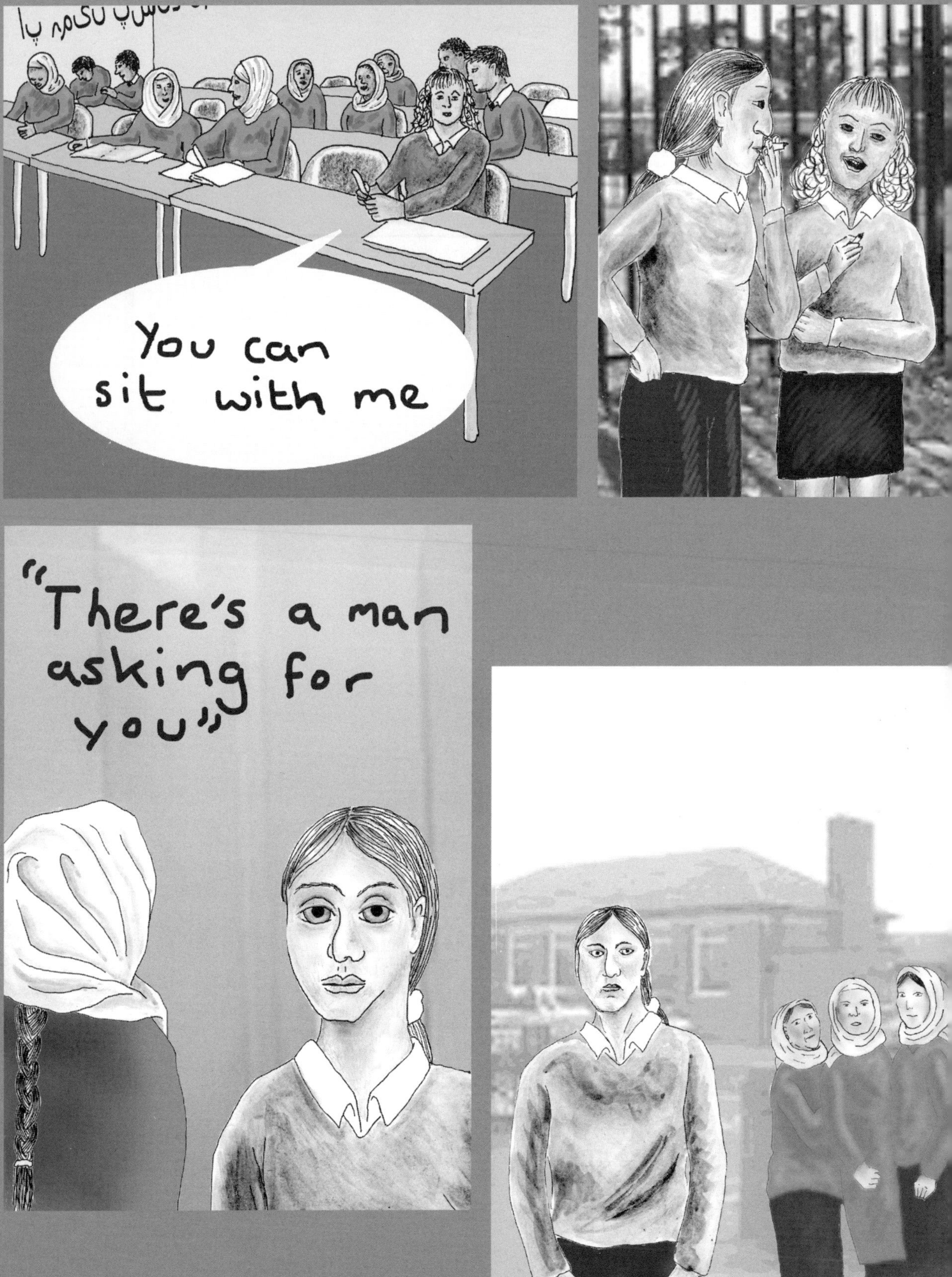
You can sit with me
"There's a man asking for you"

"GET IN"

I have no choice

I don't care

"Have a smoke"

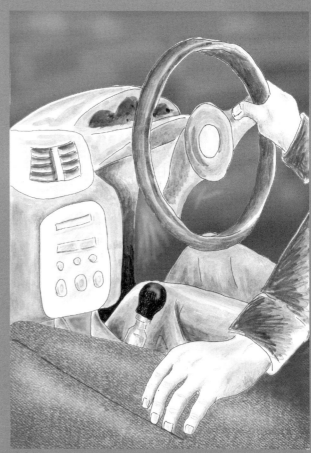

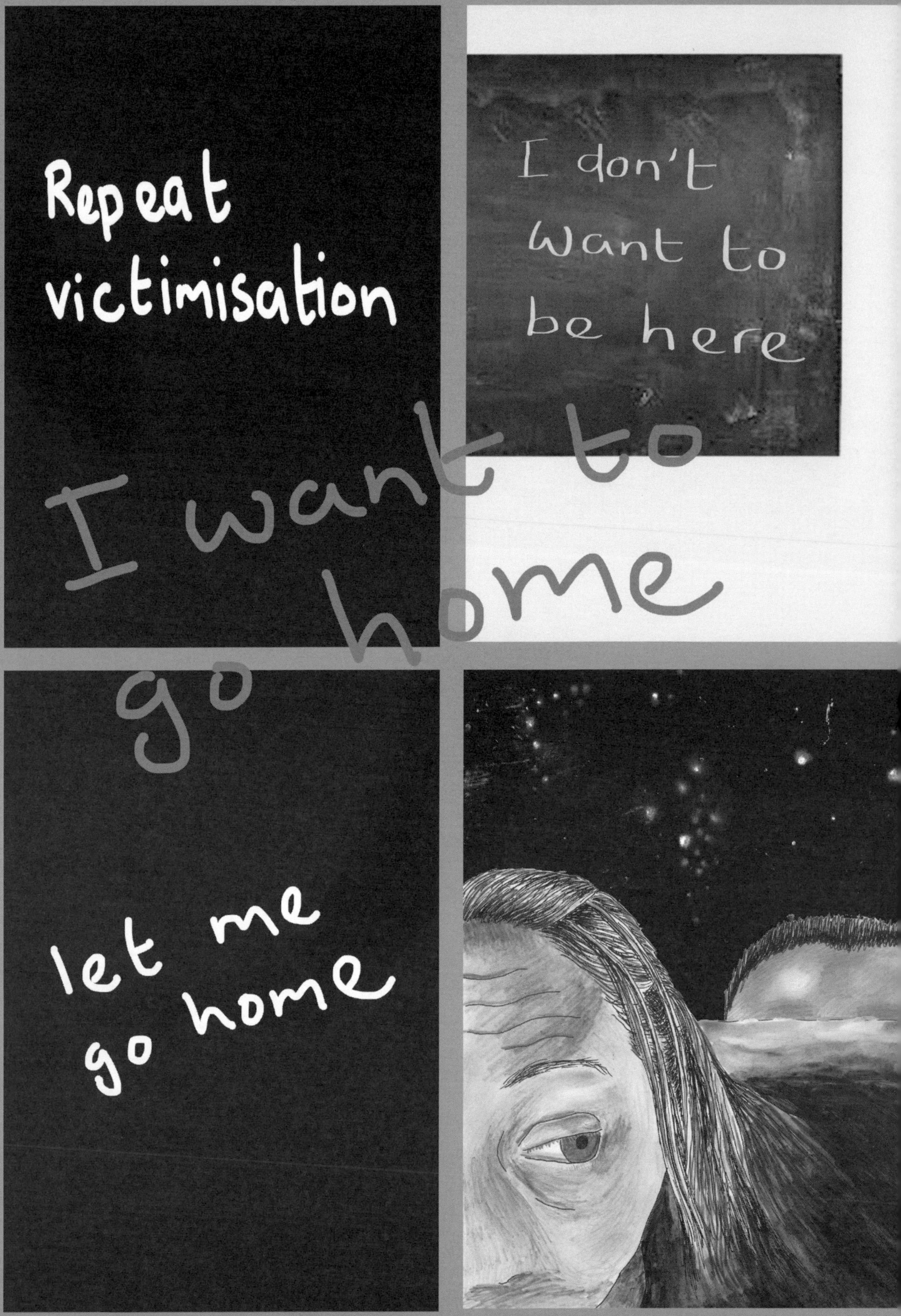
Repeat victimisation
I don't want to be here
I want to go home
let me go home

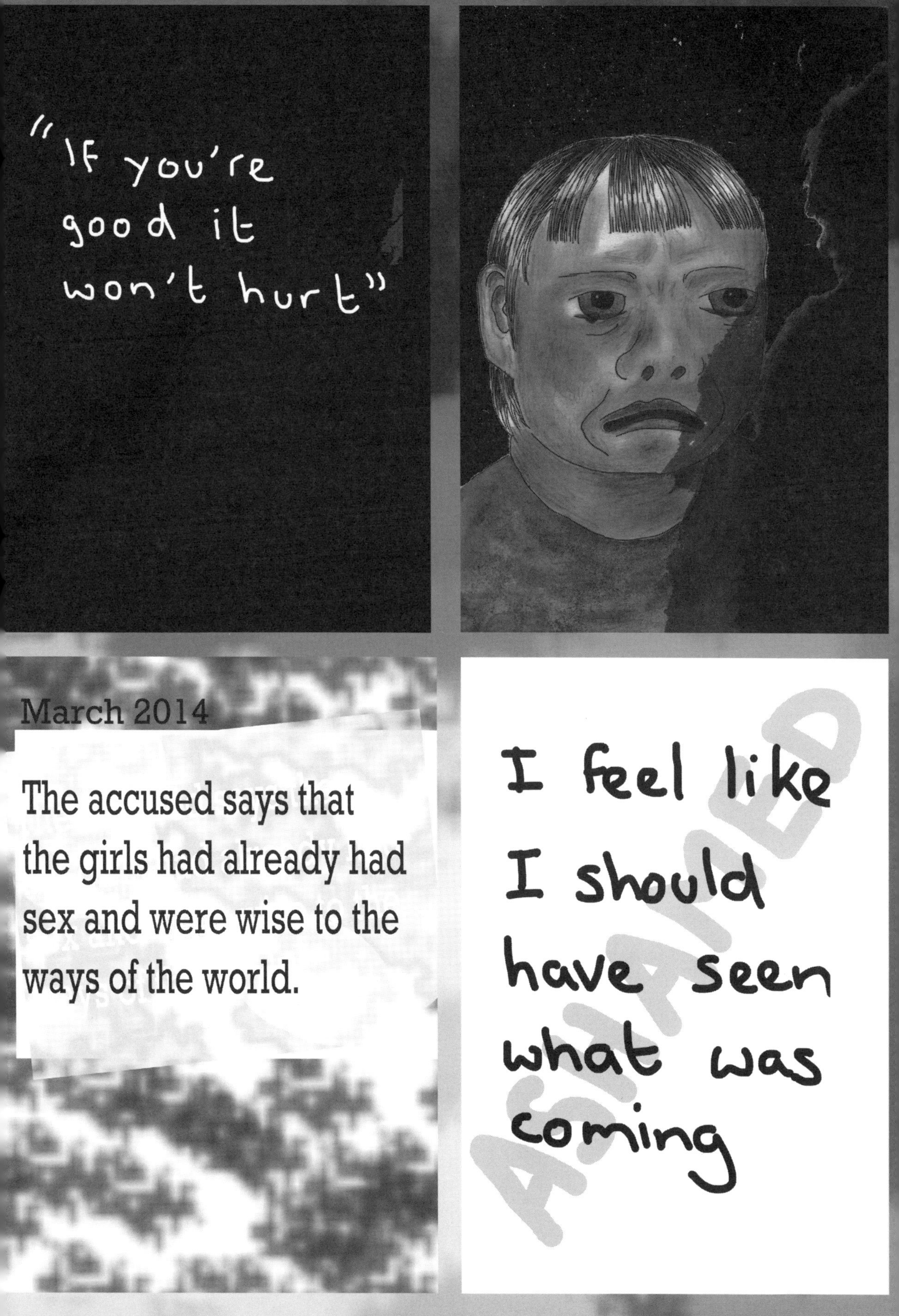
"If you're good it won't hurt"
March 2014
The accused says that the girls had already had sex and were wise to the ways of the world.
I feel like I should have seen what was coming
ASHAMED

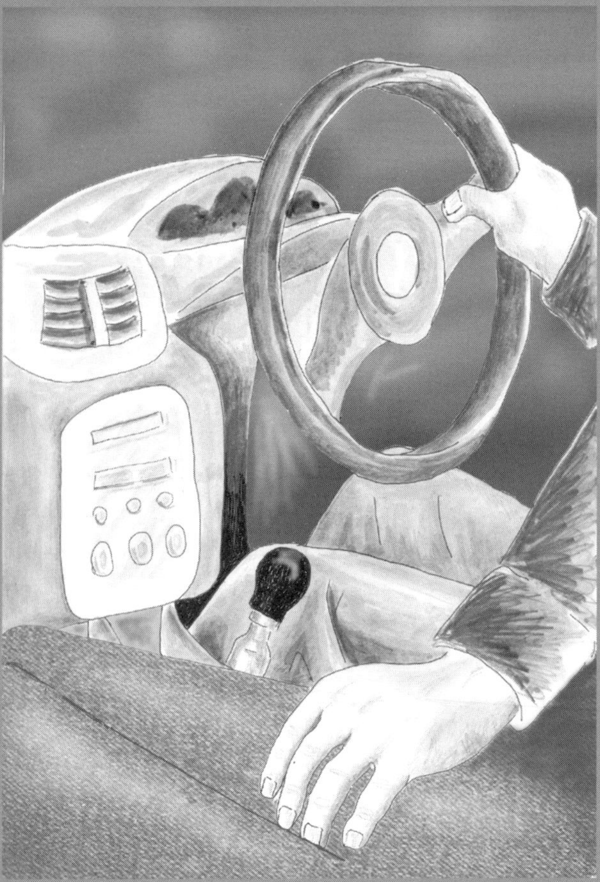

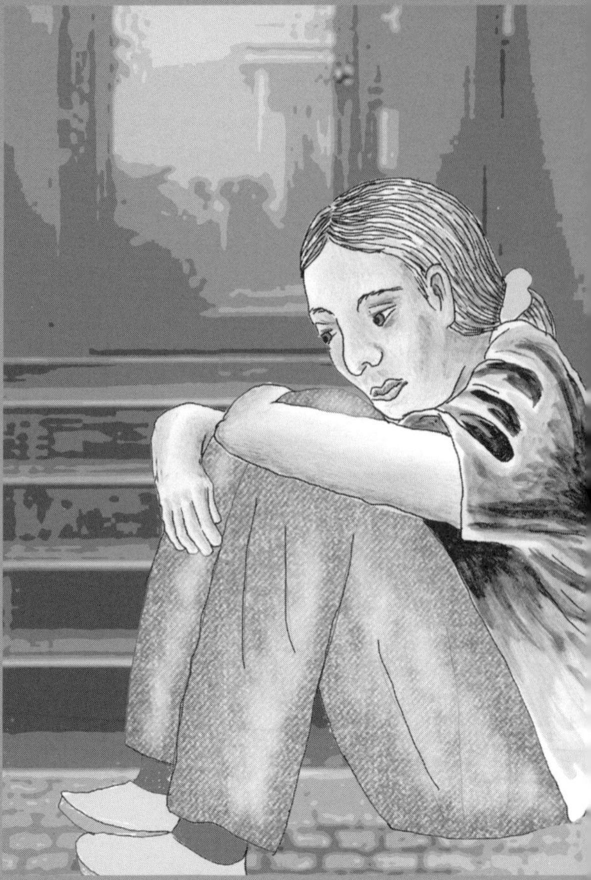

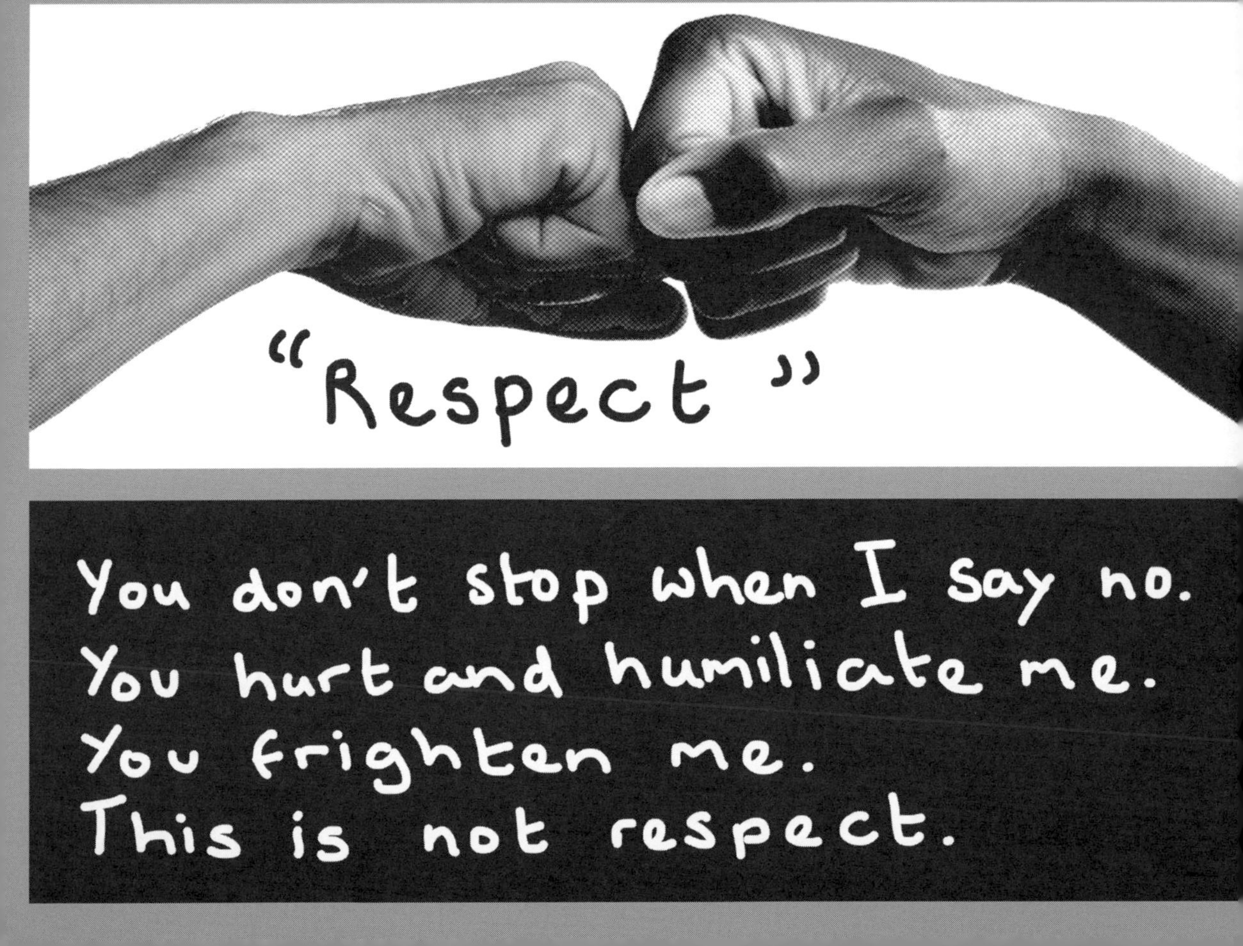
"Respect"

You don't stop when I say no.
You hurt and humiliate me.
You frighten me.
This is not respect.

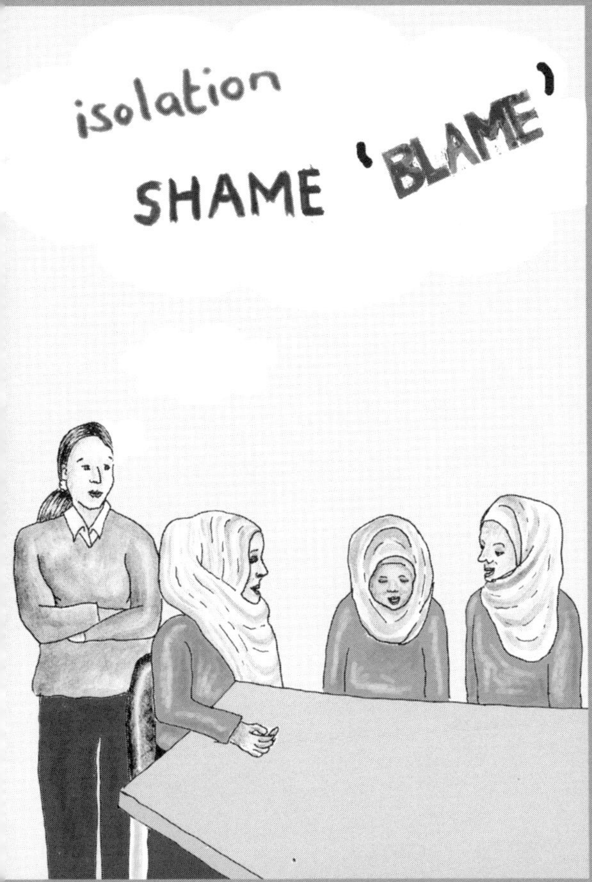
isolation
SHAME 'BLAME'

Everyone knows.

They think it doesn't matter.

They think I am bad.

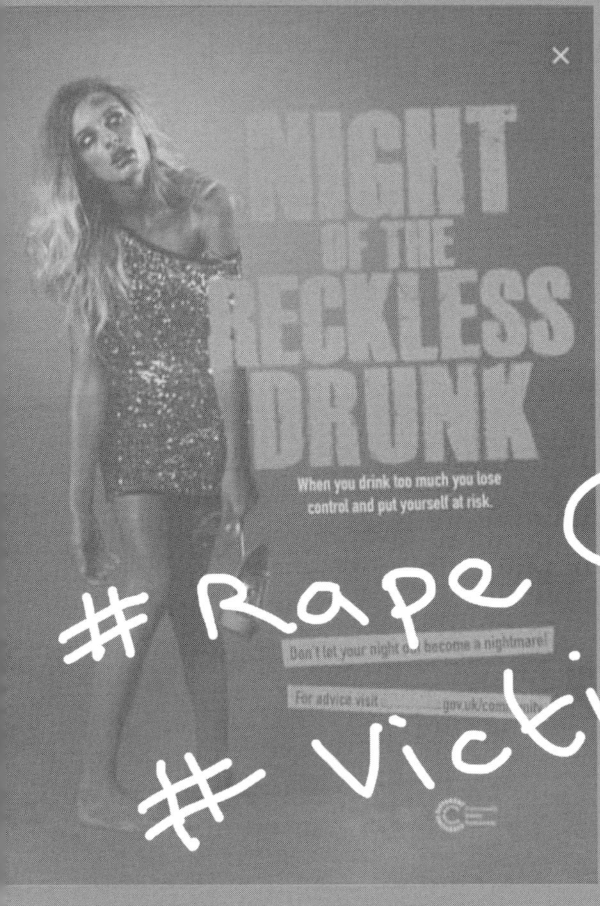
NIGHT
OF THE
RECKLESS
DRUNK
When you drink too much you lose control and put yourself at risk.
Don't let your night out become a nightmare!

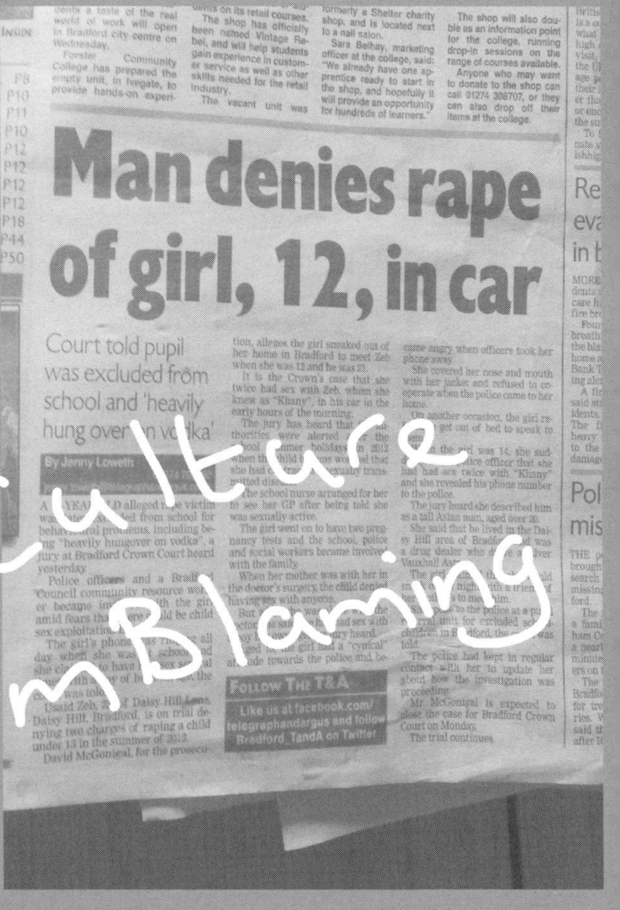
Man denies rape of girl, 12, in car
Court told pupil was excluded from school and 'heavily hung over on vodka'
By Jenny Loweth
tion, alleges the girl sneaked out of her home in Bradford to meet Zeb when she was 12 and he was 21.
It is the Crown's case that she twice had sex with Zeb, whom she knew as "Khany", in his car in the early hours of the morning.
The school nurse arranged for her to see her GP after being told she was sexually active.
The girl went on to have two pregnancy tests and the school, police and social workers became involved with the family.
When her mother was with her in the doctor's surgery, the child denied having sex with anyone.
Daisy Hill, Bradford, is on trial denying two charges of raping a child under 13 in the summer of 2012.
David McGonigal, for the prosecu-
Follow The T&A
Like us at facebook.com/telegraphandargus and follow Bradford_TandA on Twitter
The trial continues.

#RapeCulture
#VictimBlaming

How do I make sense of this?

DANGER
Who has the power to stop child abuse?
Judge Nigel Peters (Blamed the victim)
Prosecutor Robert Colover (Blamed the victim)
Neil Wilson Paedophile 39 years old
Victim 13 years old

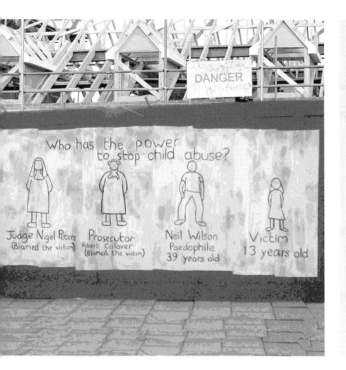

"If you wouldn't blame someone else, why do you blame yourself?"

Why do people go back?

- Fear
- Grooming
- Isolation
- No option

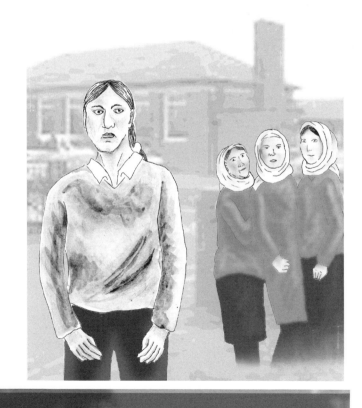

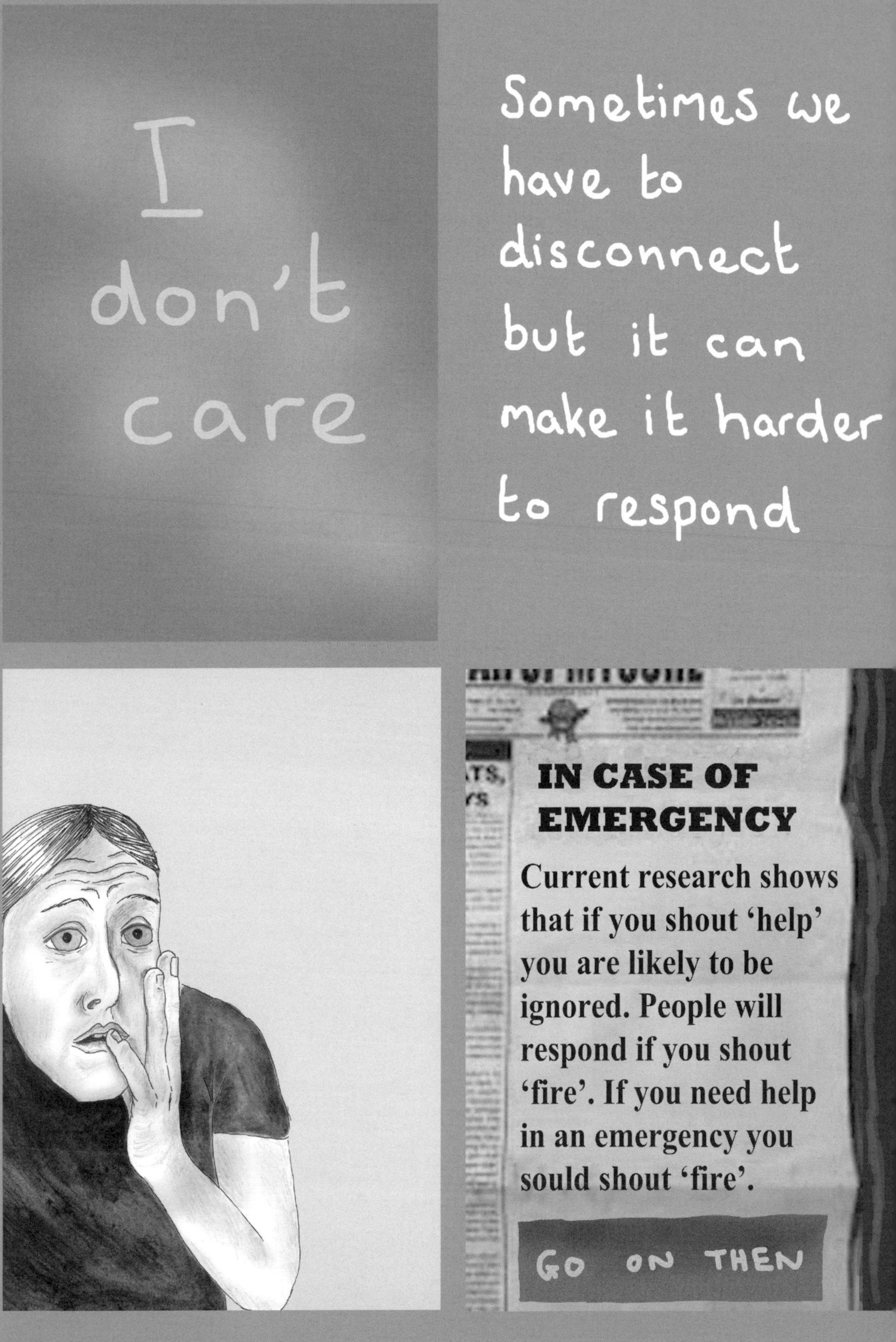
I don't care
Sometimes we have to disconnect but it can make it harder to respond
IN CASE OF EMERGENCY
Current research shows that if you shout 'help' you are likely to be ignored. People will respond if you shout 'fire'. If you need help in an emergency you sould shout 'fire'.
GO ON THEN

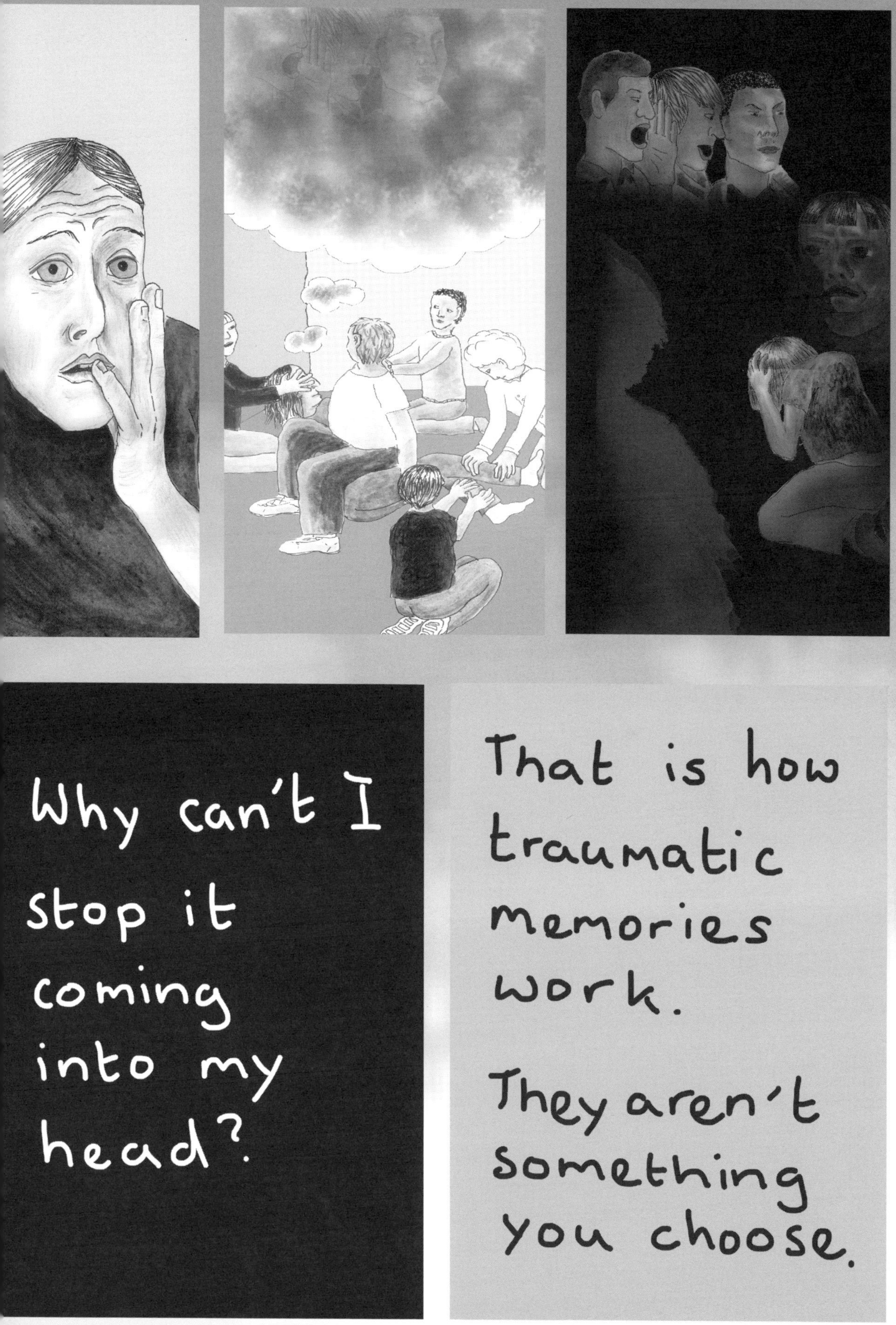
Why can't I stop it coming into my head?
That is how traumatic memories work.
They aren't something you choose.

My timeline

|——|——|——|——|——|——|——

I feel like I have no rights.

If I had fought maybe I would have ended up like Katie

|——|——|——|——|——|——|——

raped

Katie murdered

O.D.

Hospital

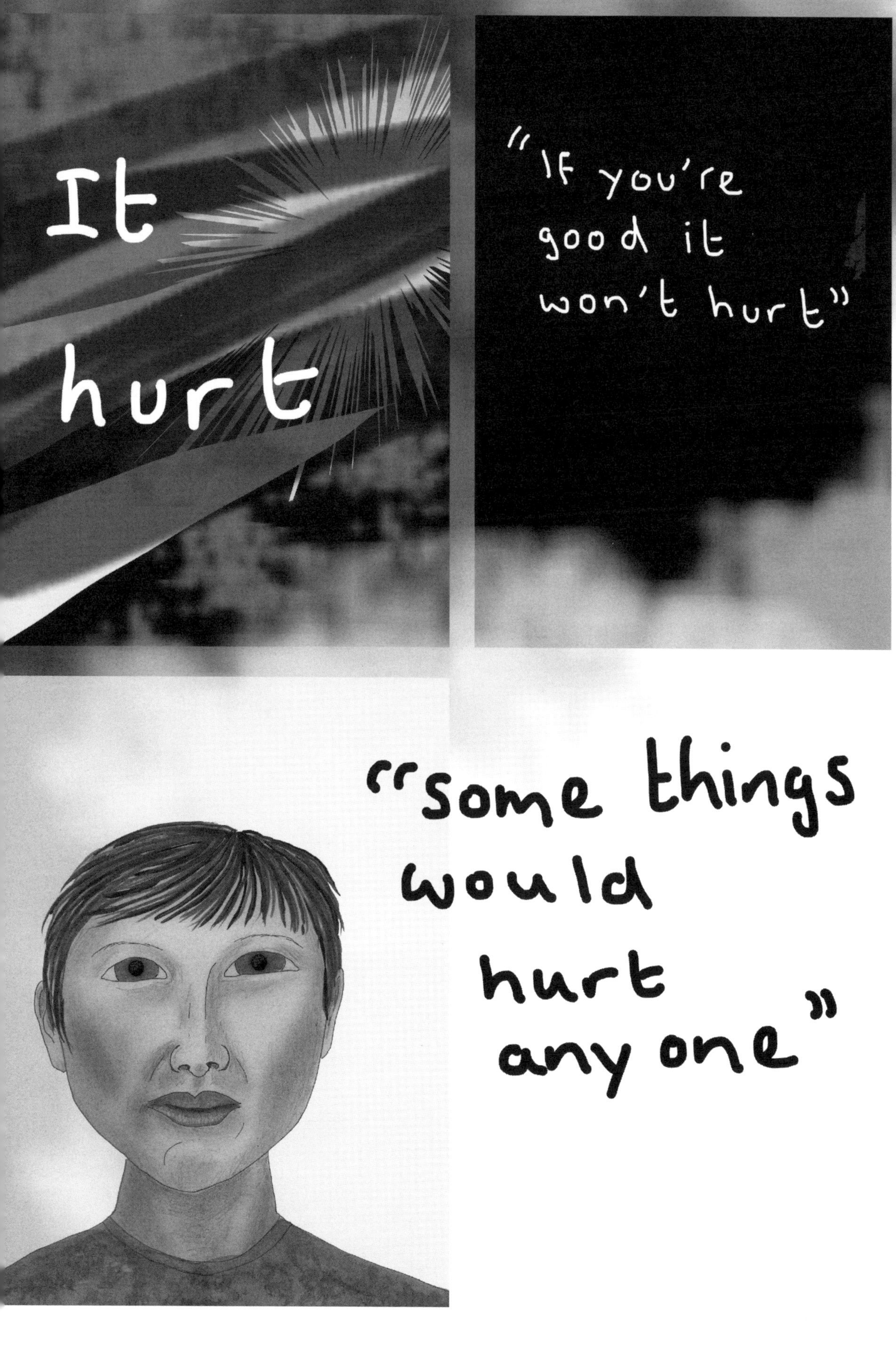
It hurt
"If you're good it won't hurt"
"some things would hurt anyone"

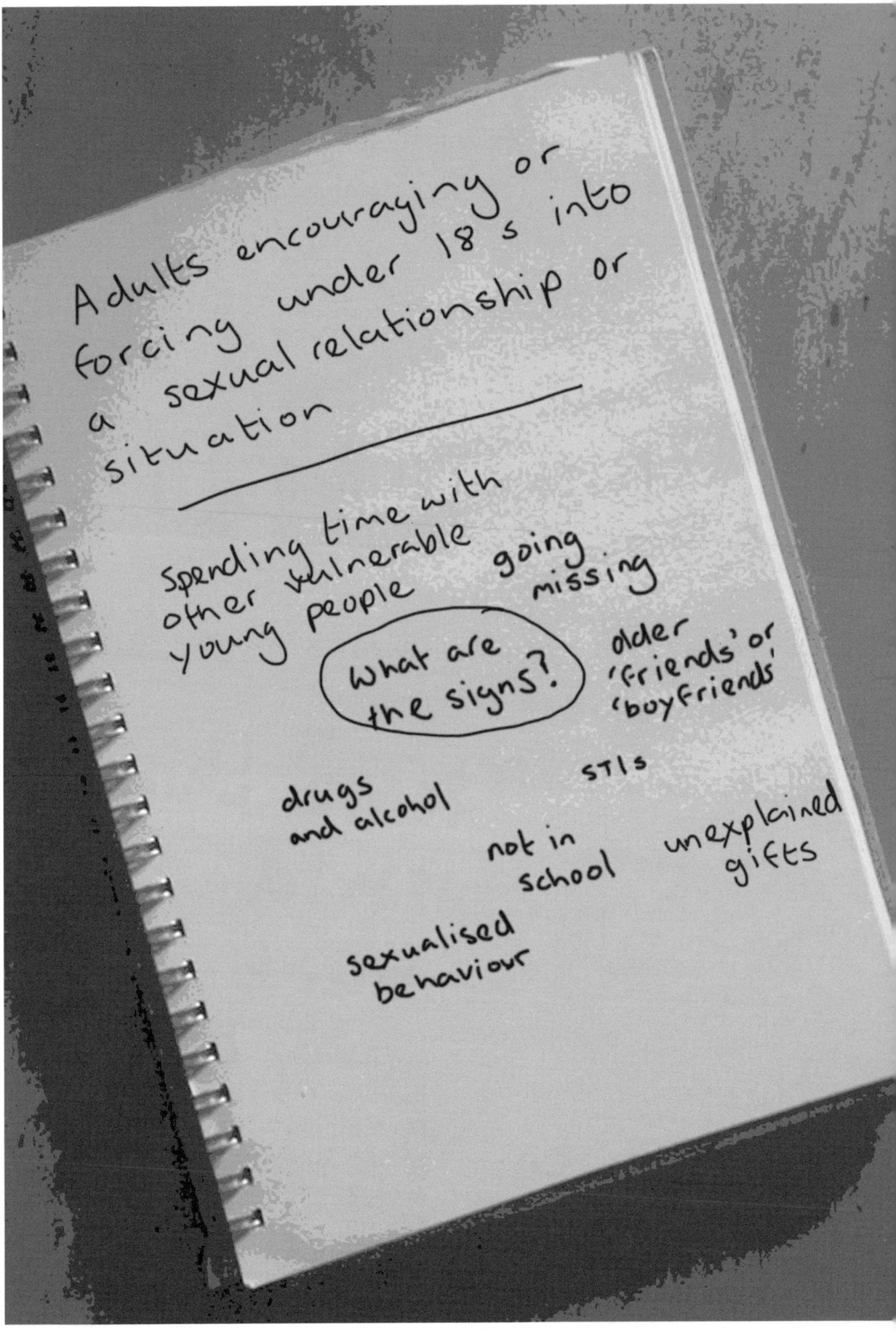
Adults encouraging or forcing under 18 s into a sexual relationship or situation
Spending time with other vulnerable young people
going missing
What are the signs?
older 'friends' or 'boyfriends'
drugs and alcohol
STIs
not in school
unexplained gifts
sexualised behaviour

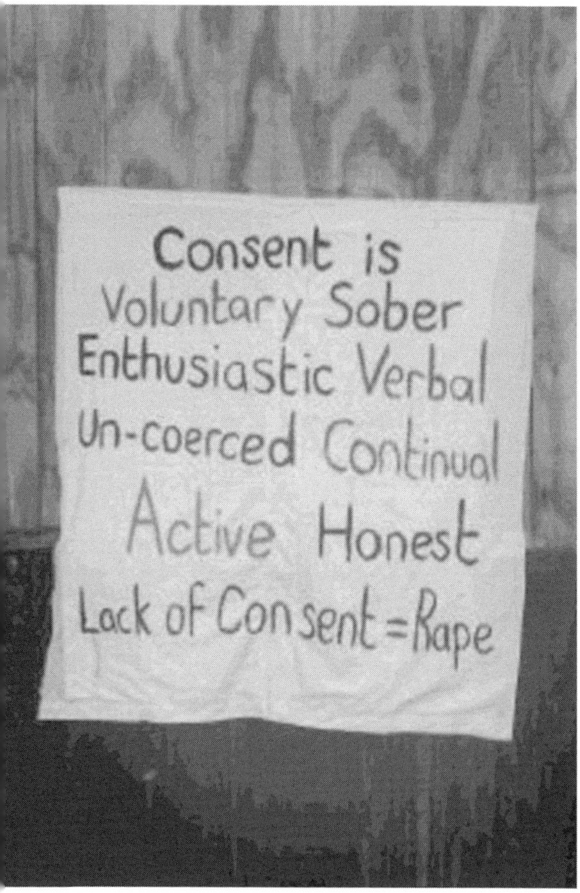
Consent is
Voluntary Sober
Enthusiastic Verbal
Un-coerced Continual
Active Honest
Lack of Consent = Rape

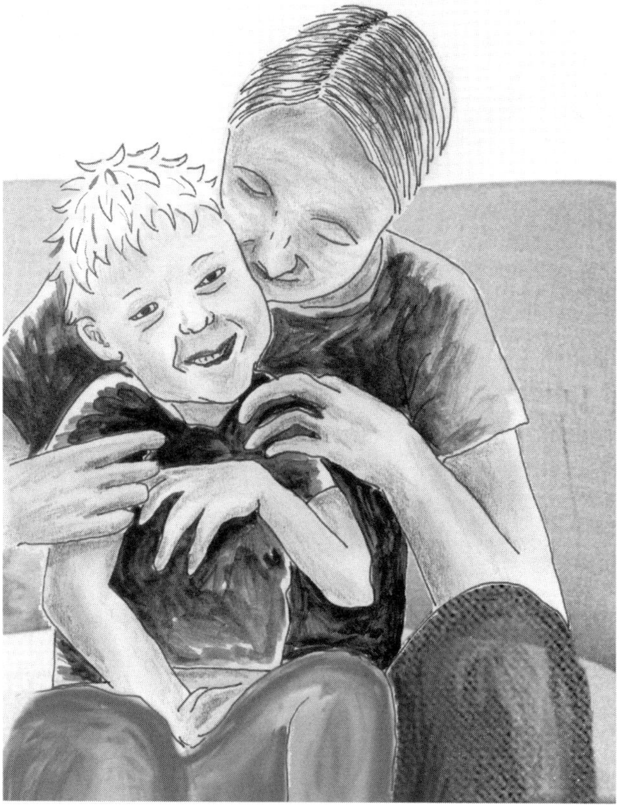

"Tickle me"

"stop now"

"Do it again, tickle me again"

"my turn to tickle"

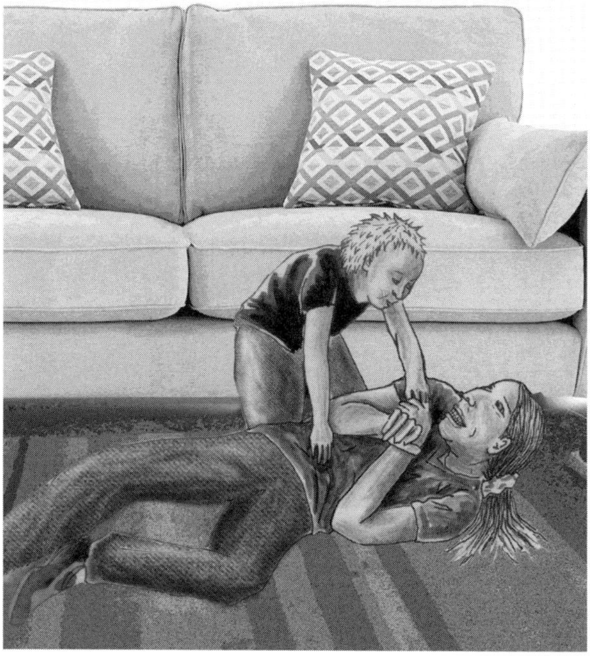

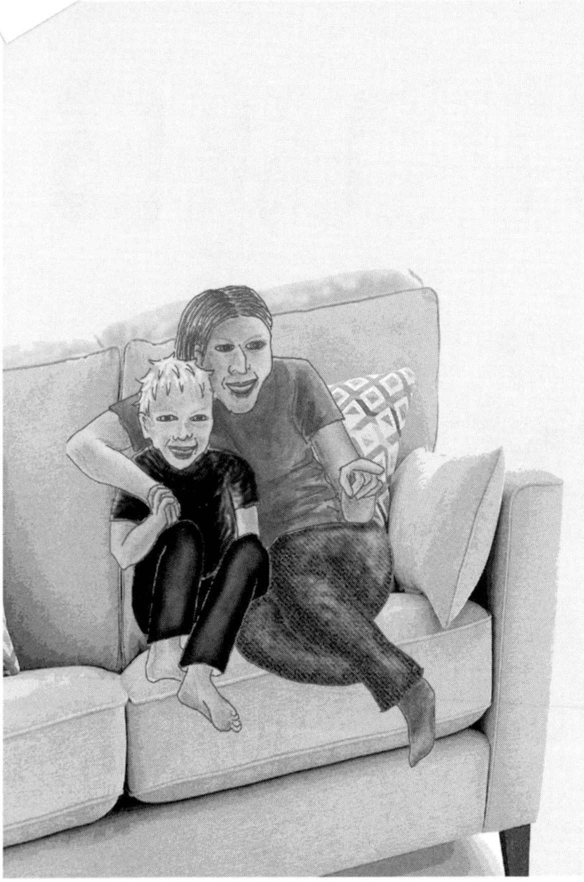
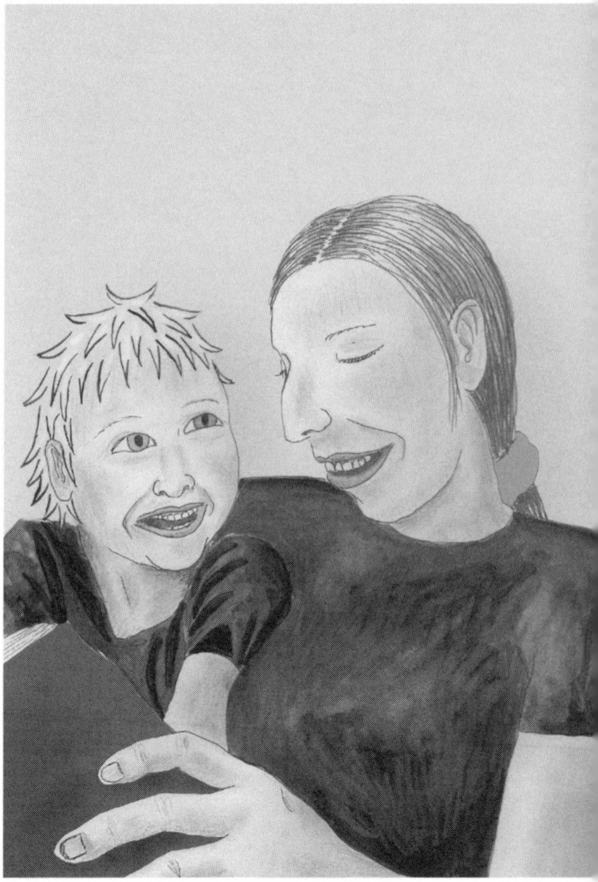
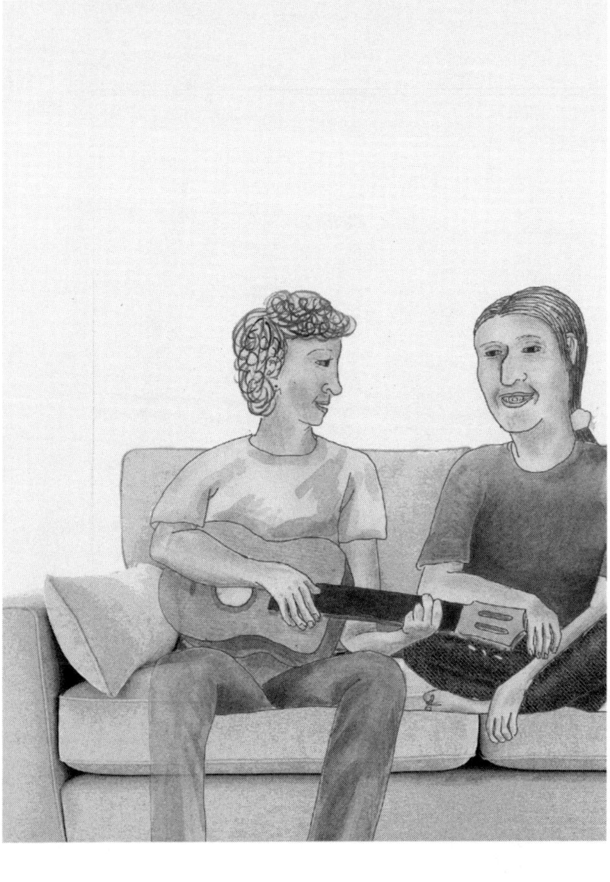
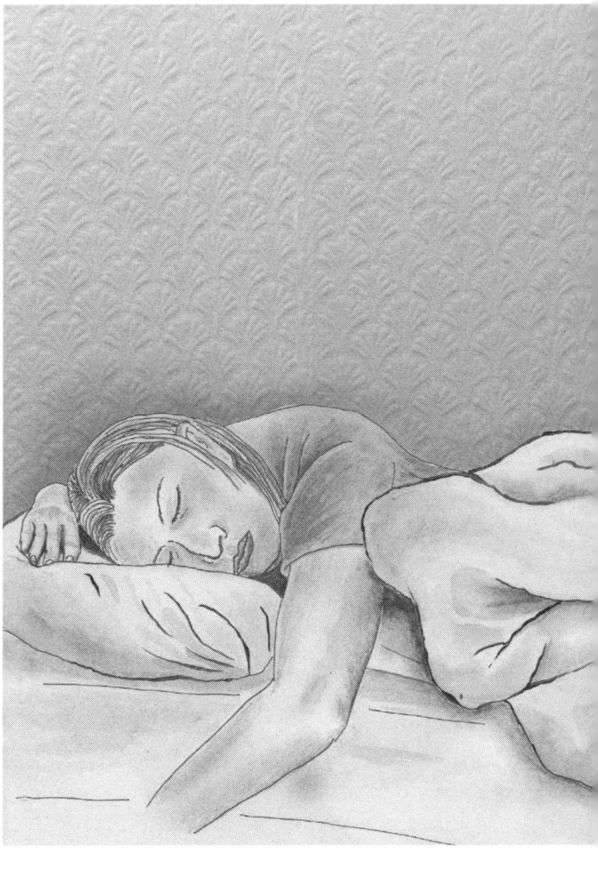

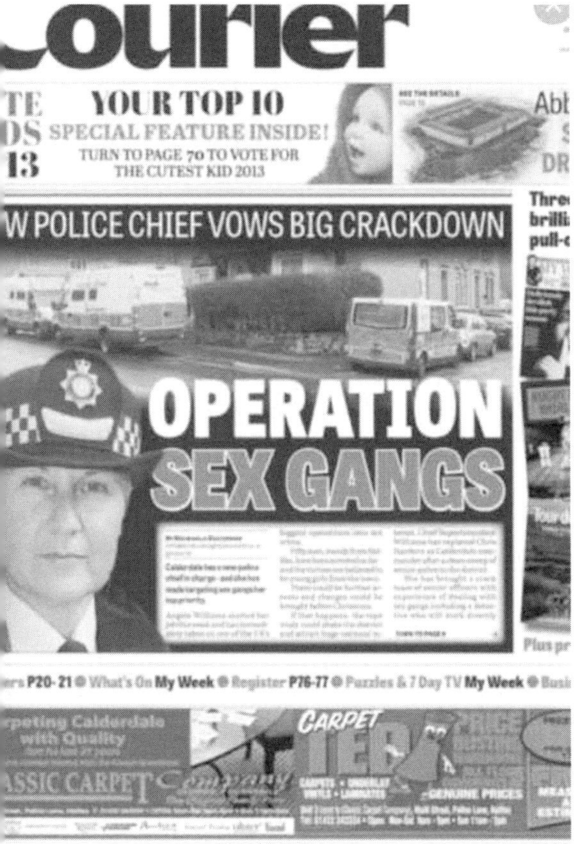
Courier

YOUR TOP 10
SPECIAL FEATURE INSIDE!
TURN TO PAGE 70 TO VOTE FOR THE CUTEST KID 2013

W POLICE CHIEF VOWS BIG CRACKDOWN

OPERATION SEX GANGS

ers P20-21 ● What's On My Week ● Register P76-77 ● Puzzles & 7 Day TV My Week ● Busi

rpeting Calderdale with Quality
CARPET
ASSIC CARPET Company
GENUINE PRICES

IT MAKES ME SO ANGRY

Why didn't they protect children before?. Why are people still blaming victims ?

I should just be pleased that they are protecting kids. But if they can do that now why not before?.

GP letter to CAMHS*

which she did not wish to discuss. I believe she is doing o.k. at School, although I suspect that [redacted]e, with its reputation of being 80+% Asian, is probably not the best of choice to receive senior School education, as she is already disturbed. [redacted] denies ...

Translation:

This girl is vulnerable. We all know that there is sexual exploitation happening to the girls at this school but instead of saying that, I am going to suggest she shouldn't go there because so many of the other students are Asian. Why talk about sexual exploitation when I have the opportunity to be racist and avoid the issue in a way which means that nobody will feel able to talk about what is happening without appearing racist?

General Hospital letter to GP

On admission to the ward she was withdrawn and reluctant to be seen or examined by a male doctor. She merely had blood tests taken to check for Paracetamol and salicylate levels, which came back normal.

Translation:

What's all the fuss about? All girls should be fine about being examined by a male doctor, however distressed they are, or however recently they have been assaulted. She chose to be here in the first place with her attention-seeking overdoses. I am only trying to do my job.

CAMHS letter to GP

This Service has been working with [redacted] and her parents for over a year now and there were serious concerns about [redacted] even prior to the rape. Our hypothesis has always been that [redacted]'s parents have difficulty intervening in her life as parents, ...

Translation:

She was already fucked up. We blame the parents. Any rapes, assaults or exploitation are just irrelevant and we don't want to know about what is happening to her now.

Psychiatric Hospital letter to GP

1996 when [redacted] had been out with friends ... to find the handbag and the next the parents knew was thirty six hours later when she had been attending [redacted] Casualty having cut herself. They wondered whether at this point she had been kidnapped.

Translation:

Her parents think she was abducted. We're not interested in considering this possibility as it is clearly ridiculous.

*CAMHS – Child & Adolescent Mental Health Service

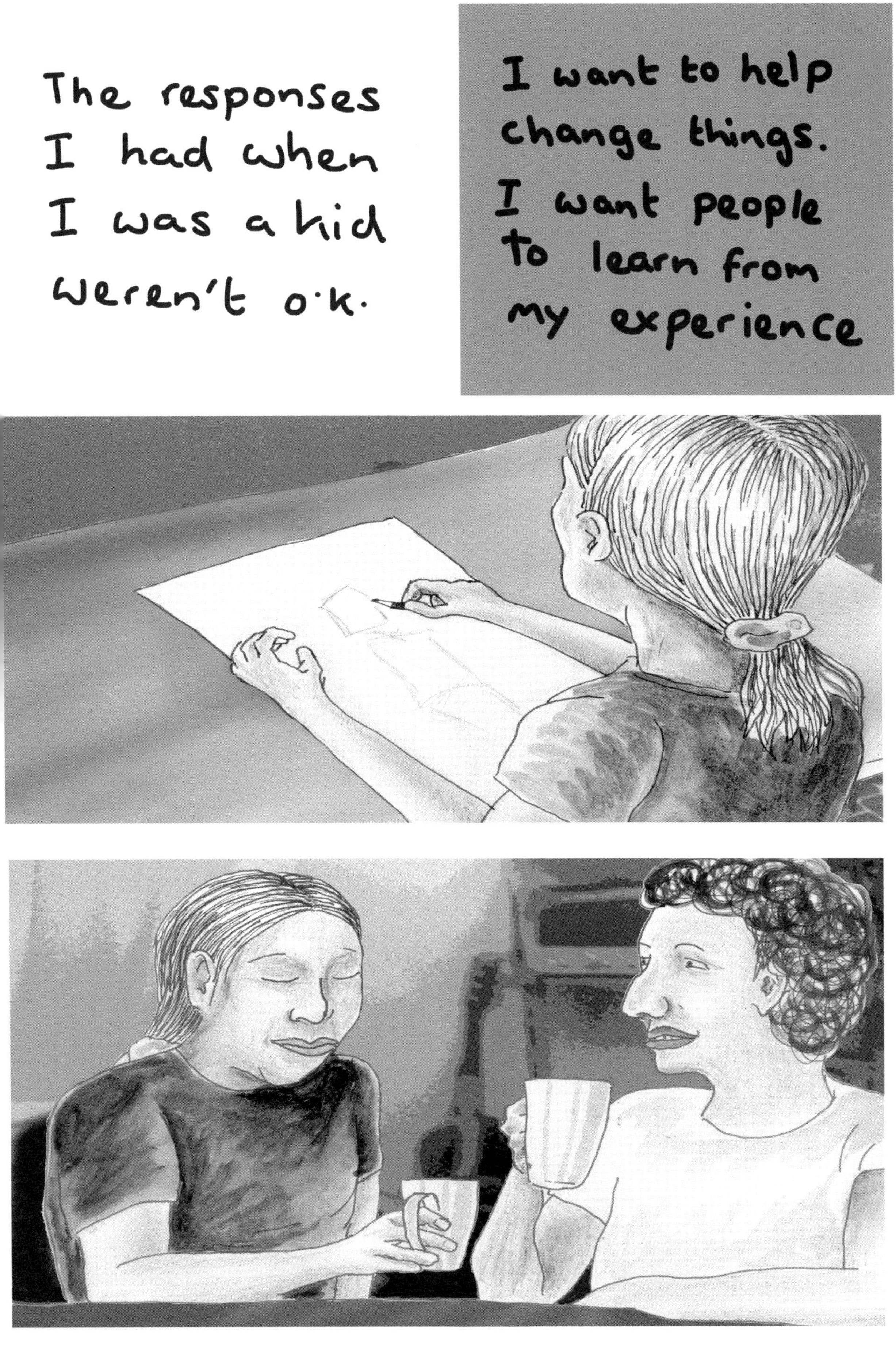
The responses I had when I was a kid weren't o.k.
I want to help change things. I want people to learn from my experience

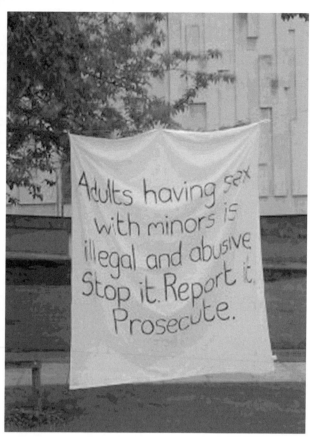

Adults having sex with minors is illegal and abusive. Stop it. Report it. Prosecute.

Pornography. Is this the sex and relationship education we want for our children?

what is consent?

#schoolsSafeForGirls
#consent

THE MAJORITY OF RAPE AND SEXUAL ABUSE CASES DON'T EVEN GET REPORTED

It made me mad, now nobody will believe me

I was hitching I knew there was no point telling the police

I was in care, nobody cared

He killed me before I told

It's bad for my reputation when my victims tell

My mum didn't believe me

It was my word against his

10 tonne LIES   10 tonne PRIVILEGE

DON'T MAKE THE LEGAL SYSTEM ANY WORSE FOR VICTIMS

I Believe Her

CONSENT

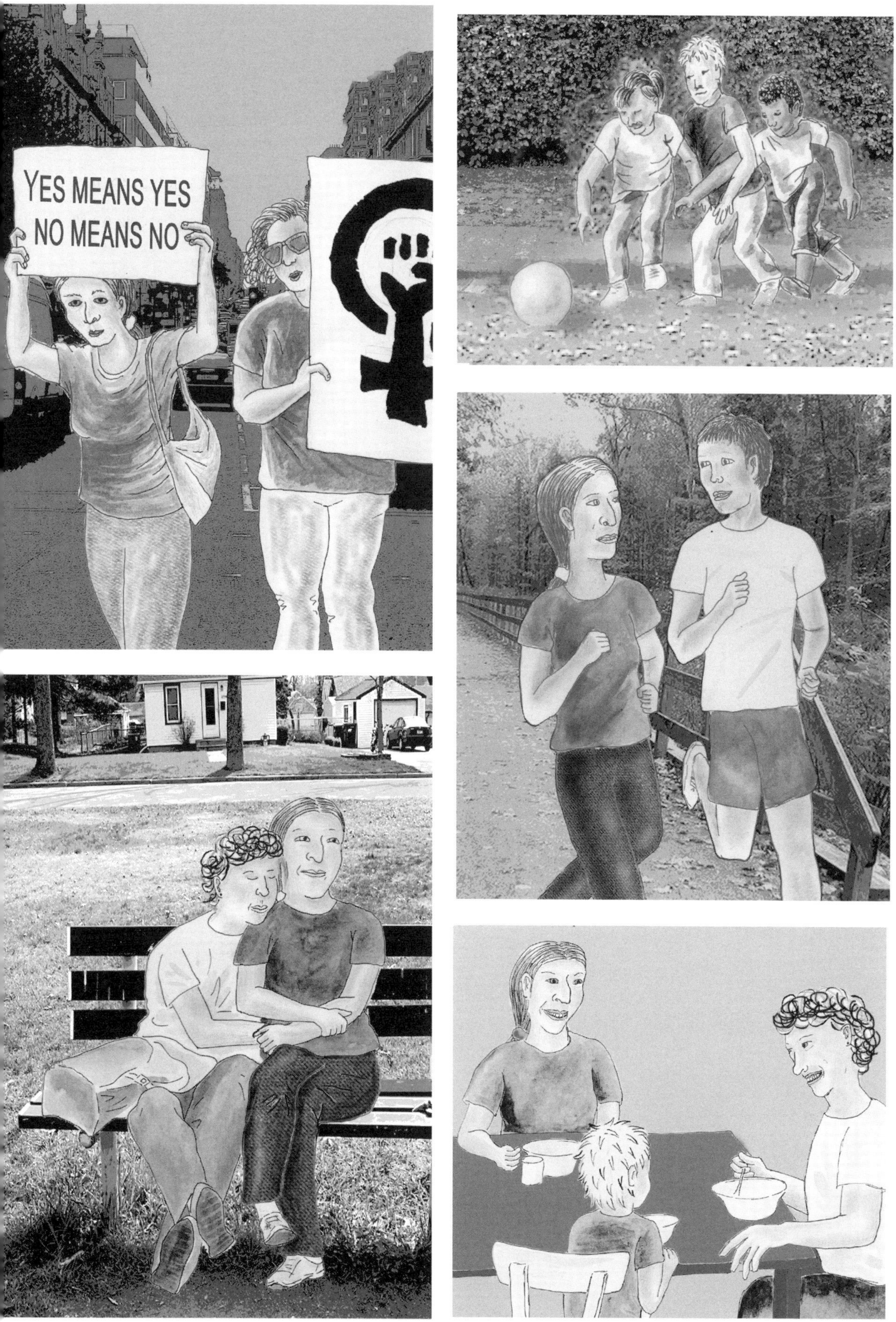
YES MEANS YES
NO MEANS NO

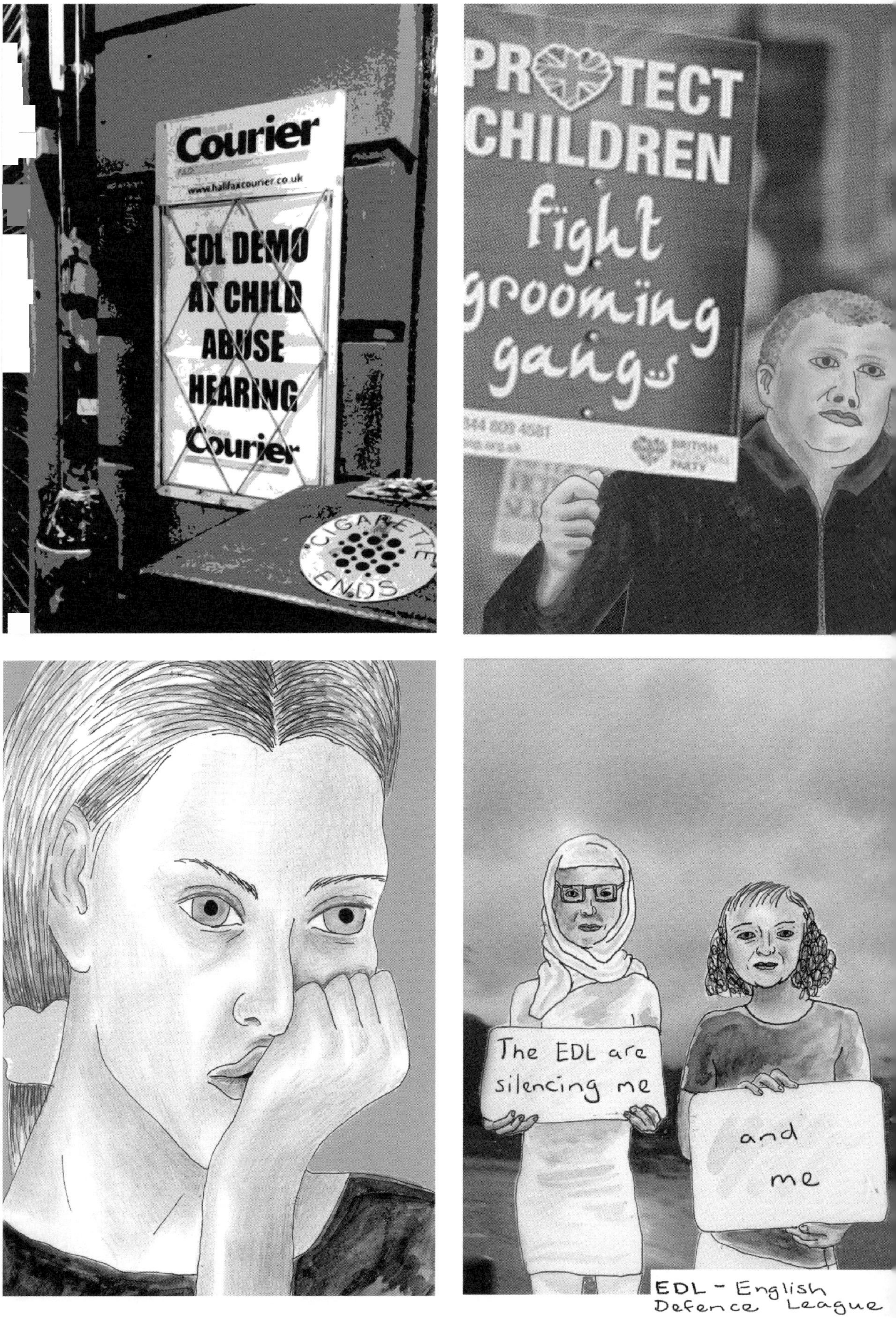
Courier
www.halifaxcourier.co.uk
EDL DEMO AT CHILD ABUSE HEARING
Courier
CIGARETTE ENDS
PROTECT CHILDREN
fight grooming gangs
The EDL are silencing me
and me
EDL - English Defence League

and me

If you align fighting rape with being racist then you silence victims. Victims come from all races. Perpetrators come from all races.

Also...

It's not anti-Christian to challenge misogyny and abuse that takes place in church institutions. It's not homophobic to fight against exploitation by people who are gay. It's not racist to arrest perpetrators from ethnic minorities.

It is anti-Christian / homophobic / racist NOT to do these things.

Rape and abuse should never be ignored.

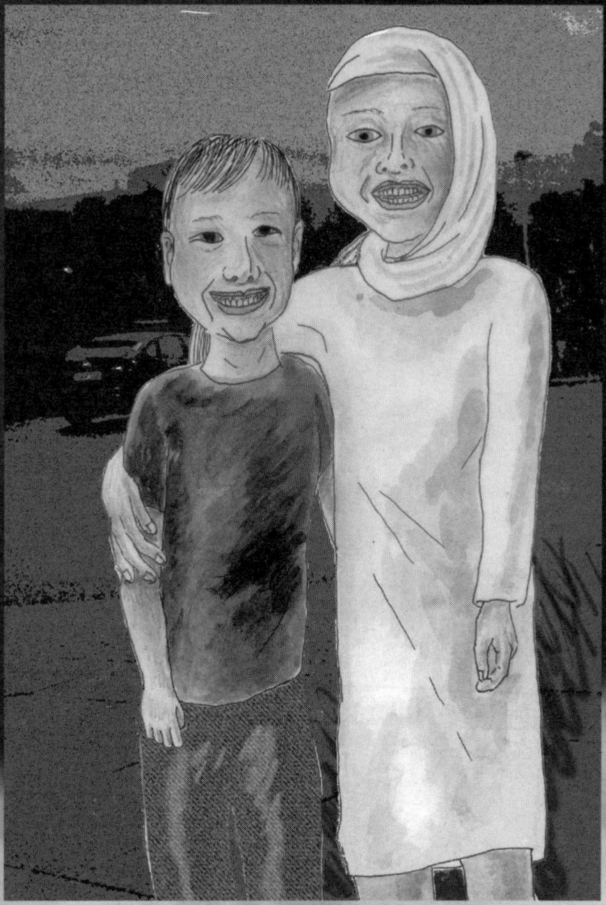

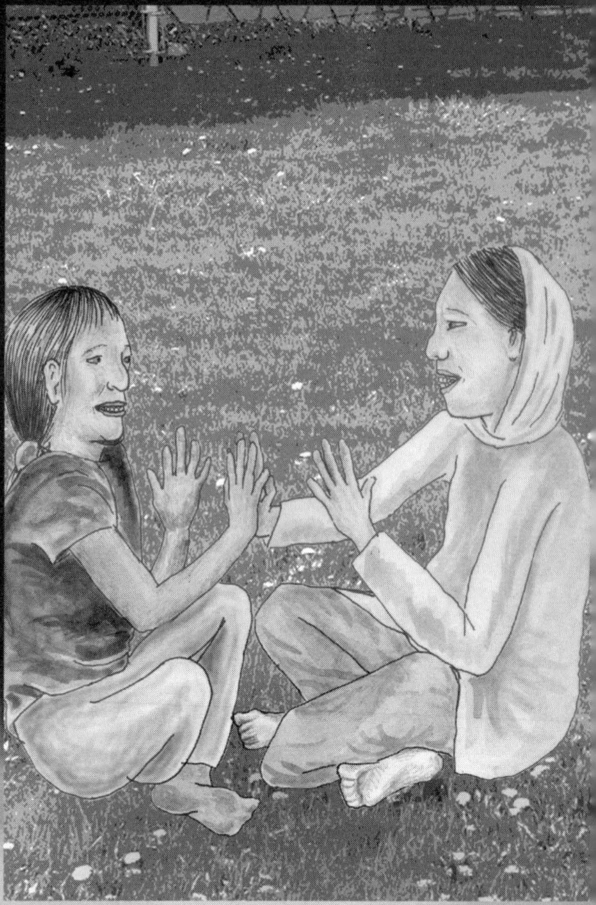

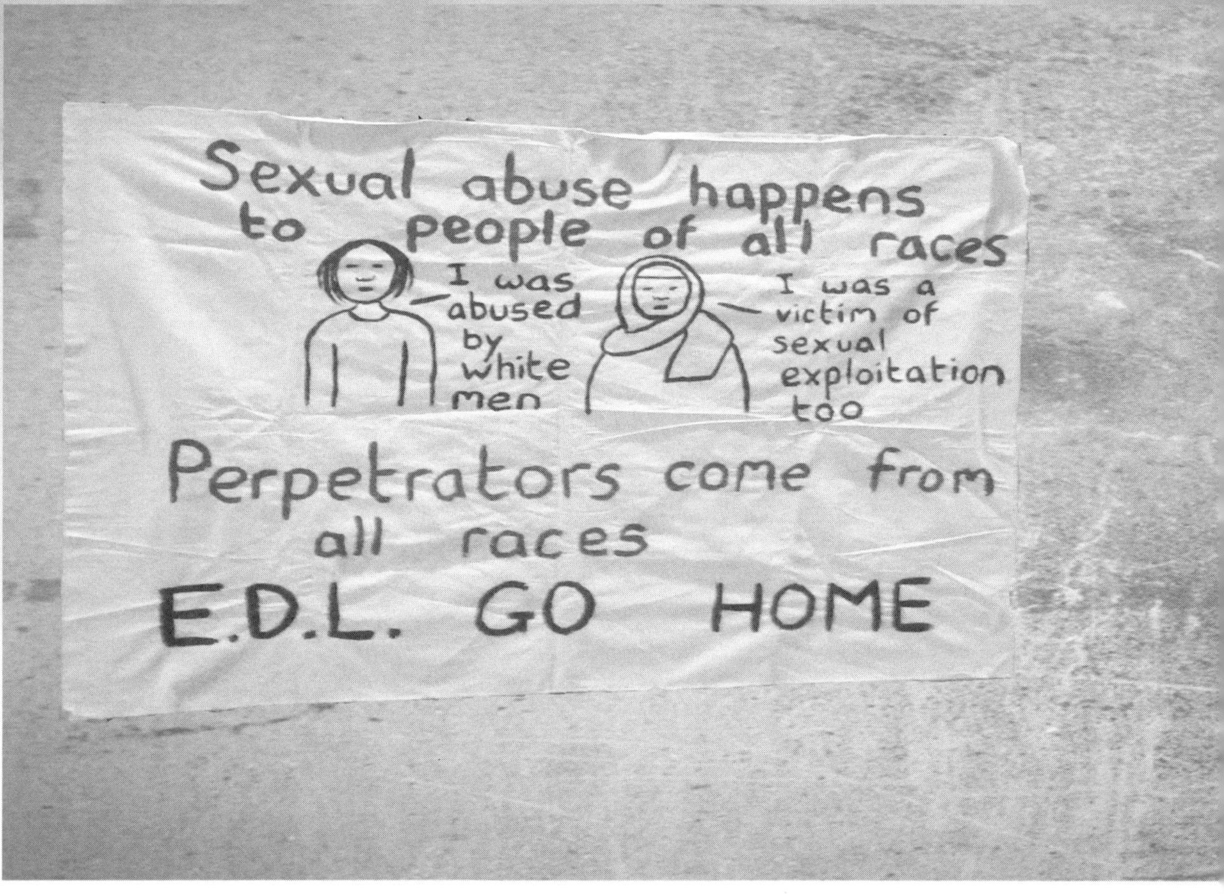
Sexual abuse happens to people of all races
I was abused by white men
I was a victim of sexual exploitation too
Perpetrators come from all races
E.D.L. GO HOME

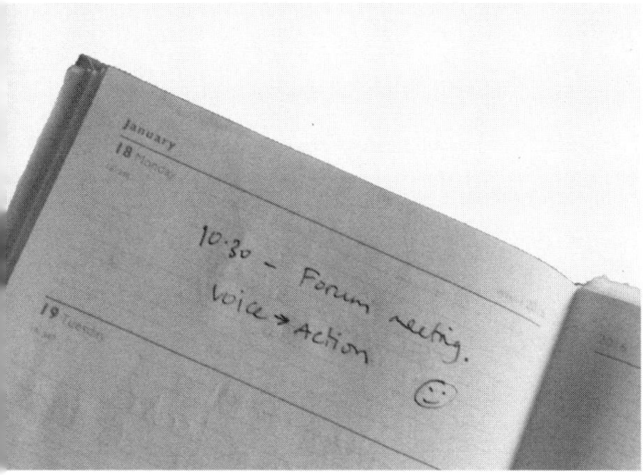
January
18 Monday
10.30 – Forum meeting.
Voice → Action
19 Tuesday

There's something really empowering about telling your own story

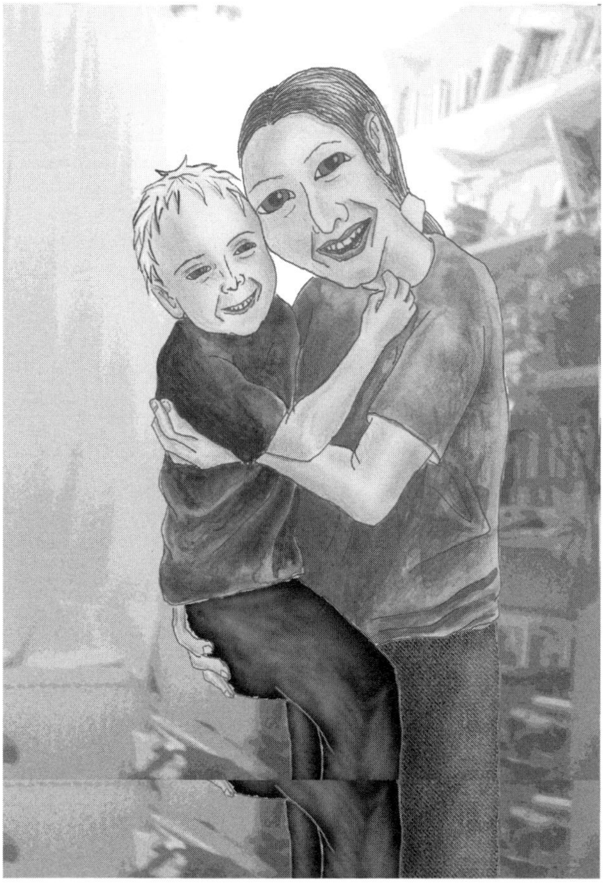

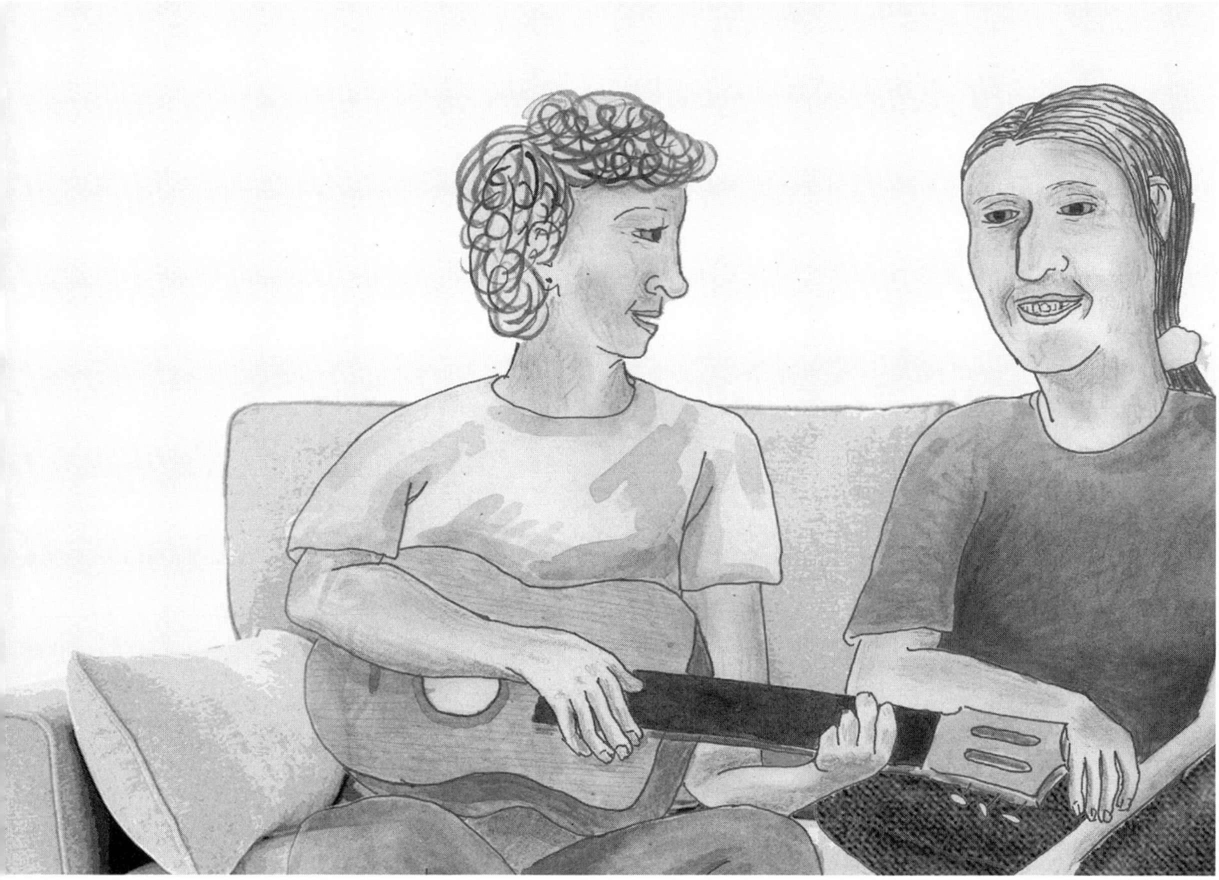

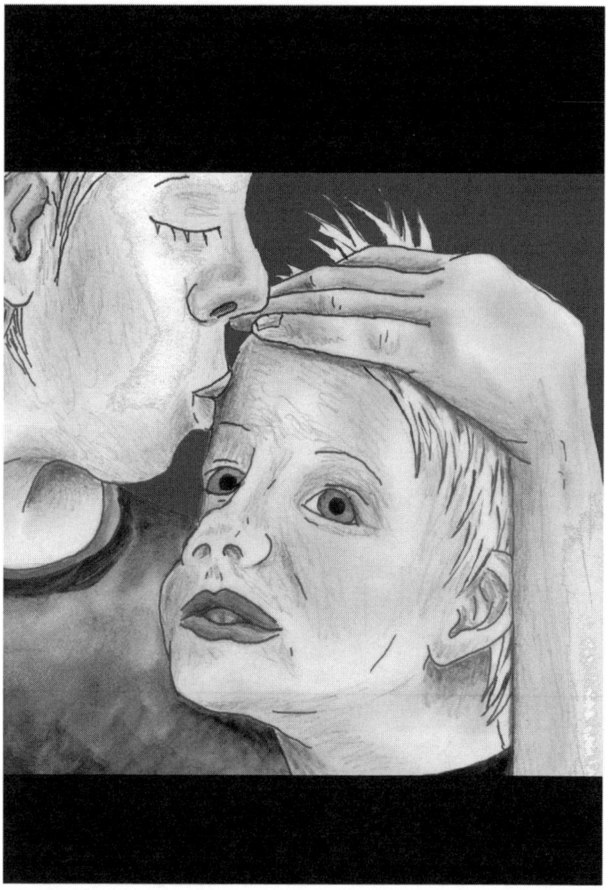

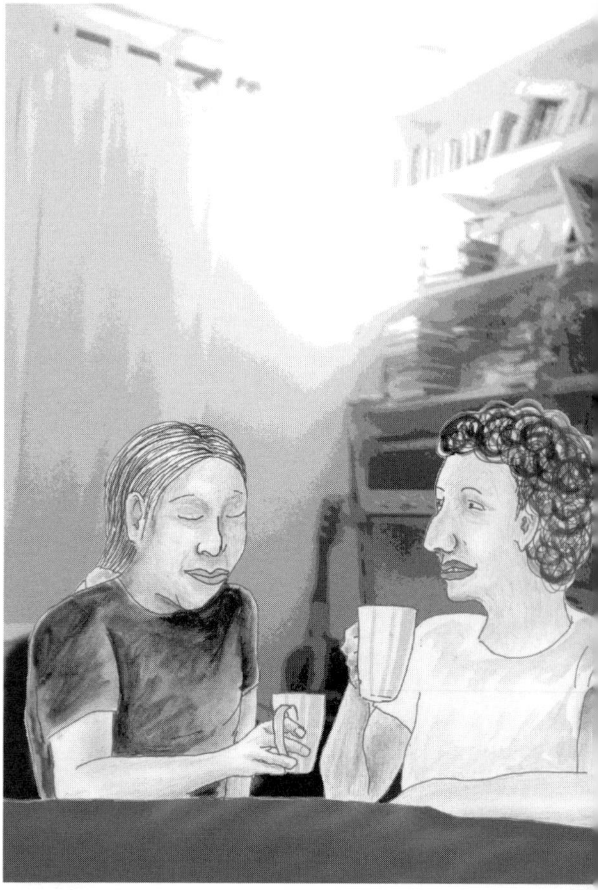

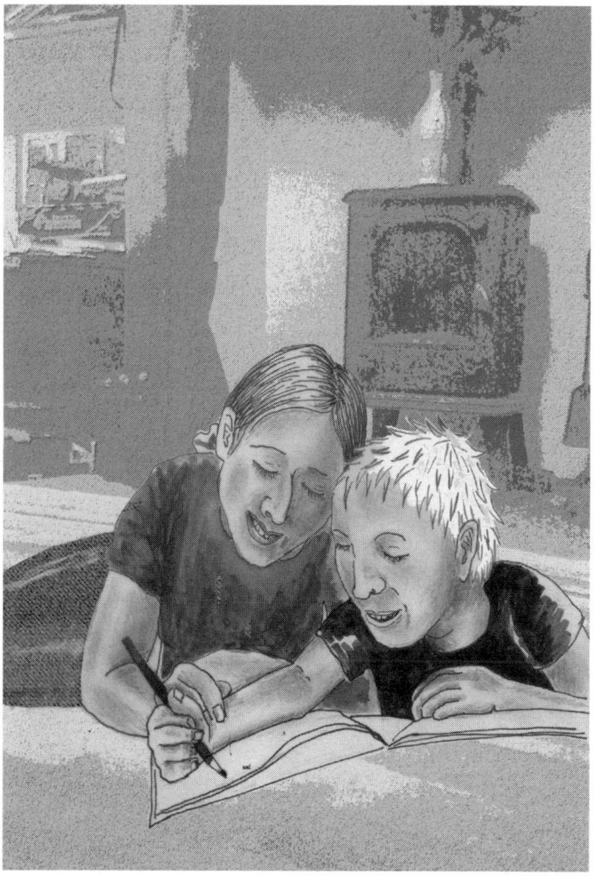

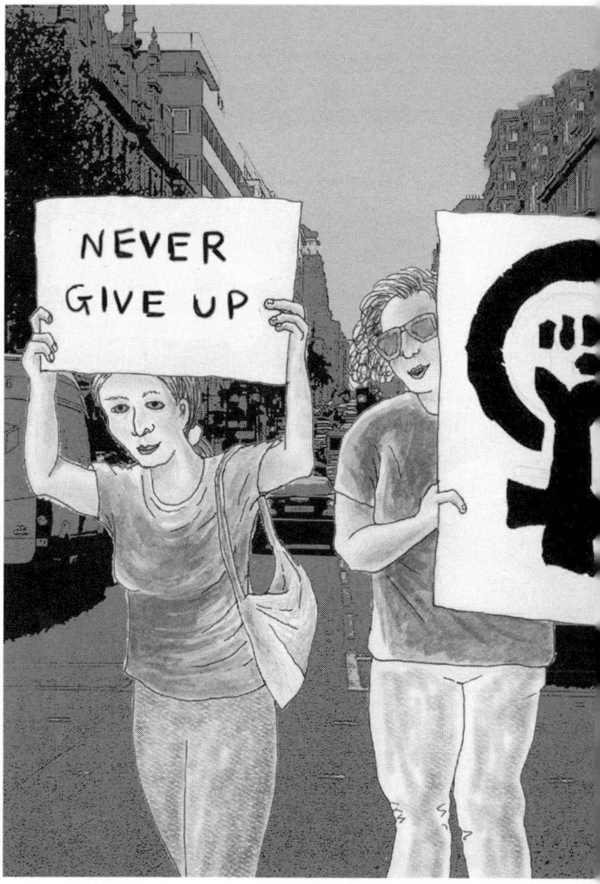
NEVER
GIVE UP

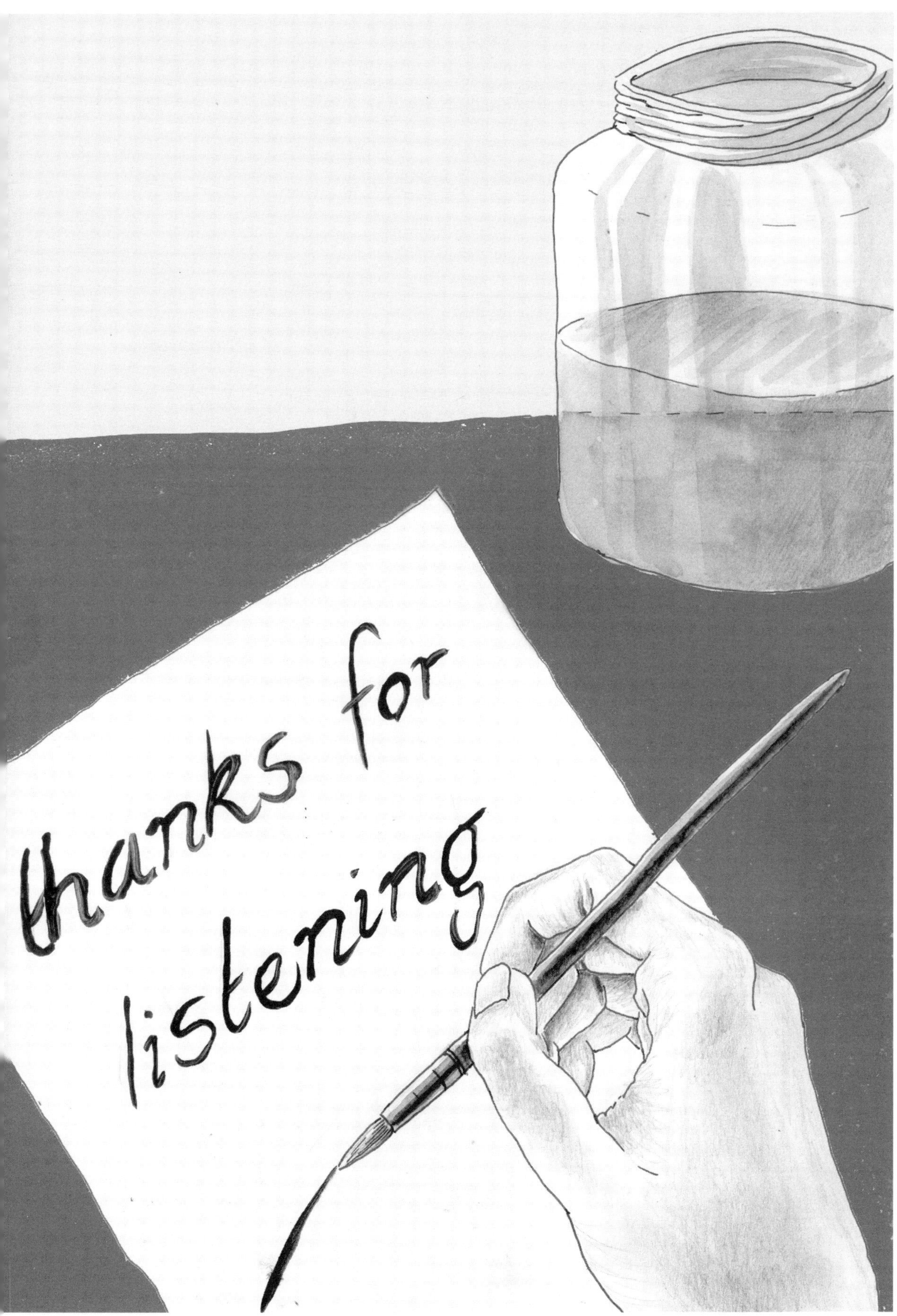
thanks for
listening

First published in 2017
by Singing Dragon
an imprint of Jessica Kingsley Publishers
73 Collier Street
London N1 9BE, UK
and
400 Market Street, Suite 400
Philadelphia, PA 19106, USA

www.singingdragon.com

Library of Congress Cataloging in Publication Data
A CIP catalog record for this book is available
from the Library of Congress

British Library Cataloguing in Publication Data
A CIP catalogue record for this book is available from the British Library

ISBN 978 1 78592 184 1
eISBN 978 0 85701 294 4

Printed and bound in Great Britain

MIX
Paper from responsible sources
FSC® C013056

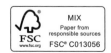